LOGIA OF
CONTRACTS LAW

LOGIA OF
CONTRACTS LAW

Rodney D. Chrisman

Logia Press, LLC

Bedford, Virginia
2012

Published by Logia Press, LLC
Bedford, Virginia 24523
info@logiapress.com
First Edition: December 2012

For my children,
Sierra, Alexis, Victoria, Elijah, Samuel, Abraham, and Olivia,
may the Lord make His face to shine on you all the days of your lives
and may you be great men and women of God in your time.
I thank God for the privilege of being your father.

PUBLISHER'S PREFACE

"Logia" is the English transliteration of the Greek word "λόγια," which is translated "oracles." This word is used four times in the New Testament. Stephen uses this word in his famous speech in *Acts* 7:38 when he tells the audience that Moses "received the living oracles ["λόγια"] to give unto us." Paul uses it in *Romans* 3:2 when he notes of the Jews "that unto them were committed the oracles ["λόγια"] of God." Peter uses it when he writes that "[i]f any man speak, let him speak as the oracles ["λόγια"] of God." 1 *Peter* 4:11. Finally, the writer of Hebrews uses logia when he castigates his readers for their becoming dull of hearing and not progressing to being teachers as they ought have been by that time (*Hebrews* 5:12-14). He instead states that they needed someone to teach them "the first principles of the oracles ["λόγια"] of God." *Hebrews* 5:12.

In each of the passages described above, "logia" is used to refer to the authoritative pronouncements of the Lord God, including pronouncements in both the Old and New Testament eras. This word, and the corresponding belief that Scripture contains the authoritative pronouncements or logia of God for all areas of life, inspired the name of the publisher, Logia Press, LLC, and this book, Logia of Contracts Law. God has spoken His logia. May his people seek to understand and apply His logia in every sphere of life for His glory alone.

Logia Press, LLC
Bedford, VA
December, 2012

AUTHOR'S PREFACE AND ACKNOWLEDGEMENTS

The Purpose of the Book

This book is written to help paralegal students learn to apply the Christian worldview to contracts law issues. It is certainly not complete. Much more could be said about every topic, and for every topic likely hundreds more could be considered. Thus, the hope is not a comprehensive treatment of the Christian worldview of contracts law (as laudable as that goal would be.) Rather, this book is written with the more modest goal of exposing the students to the application of the Christian worldview to contracts law in an interesting way that might equip them to continue the practice of the application of that worldview to other issues that they encounter in their lives. The Bible is authoritative for all things to which it speaks, and it speaks to all things.

The Approach of this Book

With the broad purpose stated, I thought it appropriate to state a word about the approach of the book. One of things that I liked best about law school and the practice of law were the interesting cases. The facts of the cases that one encounters in practice and in law school are often very memorable. The writing of certain judges can also be engaging and fascinating. Therefore, I have chosen, for the most part, to structure this book around a number of carefully chosen cases that raise topics that I want us to think through together. I hope that you find the cases as interesting and enjoyable as I have.[1]

The materials following the cases are designed to help you apply the Christian worldview to the case and related topics. Sometimes I attempt a resolution of a particular issue. Other times I do not (or, perhaps, cannot.) The application of a biblical worldview to the complex legal issues of our day is, to distort an old saying, a row that only a few

---

[1] Only twice do I deviate from this practice. In Chapter 6, due to the nature of the topic, I used for the most part my own work with some quotations from an article and a textbook. In Chapter 7, again due to the nature of the material, I used a law review article.

are hoeing. Since few Christian scholars are working in this area in our time, the task to which we shall set ourselves in this book is made all the harder. But, perhaps as a result of this, any successes that God may grant us to enjoy may be all the sweeter.

Finally, as to the approach, I will also include questions that are meant to further stimulate your thought and possibly provide fodder for discussion. Sometimes these questions may cause us to reconsider items that have long been a part of the American legal and commercial systems. This can be somewhat uncomfortable. However, we should not shy away from this important work. Nothing, even by long use and custom, can become good if God's word condemns it.

A Word as to Judges, Authors, Cases, and Other Materials Cited

Lawyers cite and argue from authorities. Thus, a critical skill for a lawyer, and indeed any person, to develop is the ability to evaluate, distinguish, critique, and learn from various authorities. To that end, I cite a number of cases written by various judges, and I cite materials written by various authors, some of which I would agree with and some of which I would not.

Hopefully this will not be surprising. If this were a book about constitutional law, I would have you read *Roe v. Wade*. Certainly, writing from a Christian worldview, the fact that I would have you read that case would not cause you to draw the conclusion that I agree with everything in it. (The fact is that I agree with very little in it, and I think it is one of the most despicable opinions ever written.) We would read the case, not because we agree with it, but because we do not and it is a part of the legal (and indeed political) fabric of modern America. Many of the materials and authorities quoted, cited, and used in this book are selected for similar reasons.

Therefore, the inclusion of materials in this book, including the cases, should not be construed as an approval or endorsement of the judge, author, or arguments presented merely because of their inclusion in the text. Further, agreement with a judge or author on one point should not be construed as an endorsement of that author on all points. Rather, discernment is needed—and, in my opinion, required. You may not agree with me on all points, and likely you will not. Nor would I likely agree with you on all points. We should be able to state our arguments clearly and even forcefully to one another, and yet remain friends or colleagues. It seems to me that "love your neighbor" requires in this setting that we deal fairly with each argument offered, noting areas of agreement and disagreement, in a professional manner. Further, we should extend that same respect and love to the authors and judges whose materials are contained herein.

Perhaps another quick example will suffice. Included herein is a good amount of material from Judge Richard Posner. I thoroughly disagree with Judge Posner's approach to jurisprudence, which is merely an extension of his worldview with which I would also thoroughly and strongly disagree. Many of his opinions, and much of his reasoning, I would find reprehensible and destructive for society. However, I still included his thinking because it presents arguments from the perspective of law and economics, which is the dominant jurisprudential thought system of our day and one with which Christian legal professionals must be familiar. Including his thoughts in no way endorses them, Judge Posner, nor his approach to life and the law. However, the inclusion does indicate that he raises issues about which Christians should be thinking.

My Approach in Editing of Cases

I have edited the cases contained in this book. If you look these cases up in their full glory, you will likely want to write me and thank me for this. Cases, particularly U.S. Supreme Court cases, tend to be bloated with argumentation and citations that are tedious even for lawyers to read. In fact, many modern Supreme Court cases seemed designed to weary the reader into submission as opposed to winning him over with persuasive argument. I have attempted to spare you the ordeal of being wearied by the sheer number of words alone.

Generally, I have followed the normal editing conventions, such as indicating deleted and inserted material. Deleted material I usually indicated with ellipses or ***. Inserted material is set apart in brackets. Footnotes are often deleted without any indication, as are most citations to other authorities. When footnotes are included, they are typically renumbered in conformity with the numbering used in the book. At times minor corrections, additions, and changes have been made without any indication whatsoever. Further, many grammatical and some spelling errors are left in the cases as they appear in the originals. Language changes over time, and court opinions are no exceptions. Of course, if you have questions about what has been deleted or added, I would direct you to the actual opinions for comparison, as they are freely available from a number of sources on the Internet.

Acknowledgments and Thanks

As always, I would like to thank my lovely bride, Heather, for her love, companionship, support, and editing assistance. I could not begin to express how much she means to me and how indebted I am to her. Her worth is indeed far above rubies, and she does me good and not evil all the days of my life.

I would also like to thank the late Professor Roger Bern for his permission, many years ago, to use his excellent article, *A Biblical Model for Analysis of Issues of Law and Public Policy: with Illustrative Applications to Contracts, Antitrust, Remedies and Public Policy Issues*, 6 Regent U. L. Rev. 103 (1995). I had the distinct pleasure of teaching along side Prof. Bern at Liberty University School of Law for a number of years before his death. He was a brilliant, godly, compassionate teacher who loved his students and his colleagues. He exuded a dedication to Christ in all that he did. He was truly a scholar and a gentleman, and he is sorely missed by those of us fortunate enough to know him. He was dedicated to the application of a biblical worldview to law. He taught Contracts, among other classes, and I hope that he would be pleased with this attempt to make application of the Christian worldview to this important topic.

Obviously, all the mistakes, whether grammatical, typographical, conceptual, or otherwise, remain my own.

And, last but not least, I thank you for reading and studying the book. I hope you grow in your understanding of and love for the law and, more importantly, the Lord who created it.

Soli Deo Gloria

Rodney D. Chrisman
Bedford, VA
December, 2012

TABLE OF CONTENTS

CHAPTER 1
WHAT IS A CONTRACT?

A logical place to begin your study of contracts law would be by asking the simple question, "what is a contract?" A simple and straightforward definition for a contract is a promise or a set of promises that the civil magistrate will enforce with legal sanctions. Obviously, not all promises are enforceable by the civil magistrate. To state this important point another way, not all promises are within the jurisdiction of the civil government. In other words, not all promises give rise to contracts.

Of course, the preceding implies that there is a proper role, or sphere of action, or jurisdiction, within which the civil government should operate. And, indeed, the Bible does appear to provide for four different types of "government"—self-government, family government, church government, and civil government, each with its own sphere of action or jurisdiction.[1] While there is some overlap in the jurisdictions, and some gray areas, each type of government has a God-ordained set of duties and responsibilities. No human institution or government has unlimited jurisdiction—only Jesus Christ, the King of kings and Lord of lords enjoys unlimited, universal jurisdiction. Accordingly, as the Founding Fathers and many others throughout history have understood, it is important for human institutions to be limited in their jurisdictional reach if liberty is to be secured and a free society fostered.

While it is far beyond the scope of this work to consider the proper jurisdiction of each of the four forms of government found in the Bible, it is useful and necessary for our work in this course to at least consider the proper jurisdiction of the civil magistrate. Writing of the proper role of the civil magistrate in his excellent article *A Biblical Model for Analysis of Issues of Law and Public Policy: with Illustrative Applications to*

---

[1] *See, e.g., Galatians* 5:22-23, *Colossians* 3:18-21, *Ephesians* 5:24-6:4, *Hebrews* 13:17, 1 *Timothy* 3:1-13, *Romans* 13:1-7; 1 *Peter* 2:13-17; Roger Bern, *A Biblical Model for Analysis of Issues of Law and Public Policy: with Illustrative Applications to Contracts, Antitrust, Remedies and Public Policy Issues*, 6 Regent U. L. Rev. 103, 116-131 (1995), and Herbert W. Titus, *God, Man, and Law: The Biblical Principles* 64-97 (1994).

Contracts, Antitrust, Remedies and Public Policy Issues, the late Professor Roger Bern[2] summarizes the role of the civil magistrate in the following:

(9) Neither the Individual, nor any institution which God has established, has jurisdiction over all things, but each has been granted limited jurisdiction in which to function.

(10) The principle of limited jurisdiction for Civil Government was confirmed by Jesus when He stated, "render to Caesar the things that are Caesar's, and to God the things that are God's." Caesar is not given control over all things.

(11) The jurisdiction of Civil Government exists in relationship to, and is best described and understood in terms of, duties owed to God by the Individual, the Family and the Church.

(12) All sin is lawlessness, and all who sin are answerable to God because He has jurisdiction over all things, even the heart of man. But not all sin is within the jurisdiction of Civil Government, which has jurisdiction with respect to wrongful conduct by man, but not with respect to wrongful thoughts or heart motives.

(13) Civil Government is God's avenger on earth, with jurisdiction to punish evildoers (those who do *kakos*), prevent threatened harm, provide redress for harm caused, and to commend those who do well.

(14) Included within the category of "evildoer" is one who does an act which is innately evil, whether it causes harm to another or not, and also one who interferes with another's carrying out his duties to God. With respect to both types of actions, Civil Government has a duty to be God's avenger, bringing to bear the coercive sanction appropriate to the action.

(15) When Civil Government punishes evildoers, prevents threatened evildoing, provides for redress for harm caused, and commends those who do well, it fulfills its duties to God and concomitantly contributes to or facilitates an environment in which the Individual, the Family and the

---

[2] I had the pleasure of getting to know, learning from, and working with Prof. Bern at Liberty University School of Law. I started teaching at the Law School as an adjunct in the spring of 2006, and I joined the full-time faculty in January of 2007. Prof. Bern was truly a pioneer and leader in Christian legal education, and I am very thankful that God gave me the opportunity to cross paths with this great man. He passed away on November 26, 2007, and he is still sorely missed. I would highly recommend to you his *Biblical Model* article and any and all of his other works.

Church may fulfill their respective duties to God in all godliness and dignity.

(16) Civil Government does not have jurisdiction to compel general love or affirmative expressions of love by an individual or group toward others.[3]

Further, in the section of his article that applies the Biblical Model to the contracts setting in particular, Prof. Bern states:

One of the ways man may more effectively carry out his stewardship-dominion duties[4] to God is by entering into agreements with his fellows. Such agreements are possible because, in creating man in His own image, God has endowed man with language, the ability to communicate with words. In particular, He has given man the ability to communicate with words of a special quality—words of promise. The essence of such words, spoken by one created in the image of God, is to instill in the one who hears them a confidence, an expectation, that they will be kept.[5]

Thus, God has given humans the ability to make promises and bind themselves by their words. Some promises are of such a character that, if they are not kept, the breaking rises to the level of evil-doing or *kakos*,[6] such that the civil magistrate should intervene with legal sanctions. Other promises do not rise to such a level, and they are therefore outside of the jurisdiction of the civil magistrate.

---

[3] Roger Bern, *Biblical Model, supra*, at 122-25 (citations omitted).

[4] In line with other Christian thinkers in the Western legal tradition, Prof. Bern asserts that our rights derive from the duties that we owe to God. For example, we have a duty to God to be chaste and sexually pure, and we have a right that others not interfere with our fulfillment of this duty to God. Another example would be our duty to worship God, which gives rise to a corresponding right that others not interfere with our worship of God. Johannes Althusius, for example, understood rights this way. *See, e.g., Natural Rights, Popular Sovereignty, and Covenant Politics: Johannes Althusius and the Dutch Revolt and Republic* in John Witte, Jr., *The Reformation of Rights: Law, Religion, and Human Rights in Early Modern Calvinism* 143-207 (2007).

In the context of the Prof. Bern quotation above, the stewardship-dominion duties are derived from God's initial command to Adam and Eve to take dominion over the Earth in *Genesis* 1:28-29 and His reiteration of that command to Noah after the flood in *Genesis* 9:1-7. Prof. Bern states this important duty this way: "man has a duty to God to govern his own life and to steward all that he is and has in a way that glorifies God." Roger Bern, *Biblical Model, supra*, at 119 n.84. This duty is particularly important when considering contracts, property rights, and other commercial or business areas of law.

[5] Roger Bern, *Biblical Model, supra*, at 131-132 (citations omitted).

[6] *Kakos* is the Greek word used in both *Romans* 13:4 (translated in the King James Version as "him that doeth evil") and 1 *Peter* 2:14 (translated in the King James Version as "evildoers").

In order to illustrate, an example might be helpful. If I promise my wife to take the trash out, there is a sense in which I have broken my word and therefore acted unethically or immorally if I fail to do so. However, my wife will not be able to go to the Bedford Circuit Court in Virginia, where we live, and sue me for breach of contract. In this example, I have acted unethically or immorally but not "illegally." My promise to take out the trash was not a contract. The civil magistrate will not sanction me for failing to fulfill this promise. (Although, for repeated offenses of this nature, there may well be sanctions within the jurisdiction of family government and perhaps even church government in more serious situations.)

By contrast, if I promise to sell my neighbor five laying hens for ten dollars each, and I break that promise, he can sue me for breach of that promise. It is a contract, and it is enforceable by the civil magistrate with legal sanctions.

So then, you can see that, for the purposes of this course and working as a legal professional in general, it is very important to be able to determine which promises are actually contracts. Determining this will in turn determine whether or not the civil magistrate can be called upon to enforce the promise or set of promises with legal sanctions. This leads naturally to the requirements, or elements, for a valid, enforceable contract. The study of these elements will consume much of your time in this course.

The following case presents an interesting illustration of these issues. As you read it consider: (1) whether the elements of a valid, enforceable contract exist under these facts, (2) whether some other theory should be used for the civil magistrate to enforce this promise even if the elements of a valid, enforceable contract are not satisfied, and (3) whether this is the type of promise that should be within the jurisdiction of the civil magistrate or the family or perhaps both.

Calabro v. Calabro
15 S.W.3d 873 (Tenn. Ct. App. 1999)

This appeal involves a suit for breach of contract. Plaintiff, Belinda Hope Calabro, appeals from the order of the trial court granting summary judgement to defendant, Arthur Donald Calabro.

Plaintiff, Hope Calabro, is the daughter of the defendant, Arthur Calabro. Arthur Calabro and Hope's mother were divorced when Hope was four years old. From the time of the divorce until Hope Calabro finished high school she lived in Oklahoma with her mother who was granted sole custody of Hope at the time of the divorce procedings [sic]. During all times material to this case defendant lived in Memphis,

Tennessee. He provided financial support to Hope while she was living with her mother including an allowance, an automobile, and travel expenses. While Hope Calabro was growing up, Arthur Calabro saw her during summers and on some holidays.

Hope Calabro had an excellent [*sic*] academic record in high school. During her senior year of high school Arthur Calabro offered to pay his daughter's expenses to attend a distinguished, private universisty [*sic*] if she received at least $10,000.00 in financial aid. At the time that Hope Calabro was applying to colleges, she knew that she was eligible to attend the University of Oklahoma and receive a full scholarship, sufficient to pay tuition, room, board, books, and student activity fee. Knowing that her father would be willing to finance her college education at a private college if she received $10,000.00 in financial aid, Hope applied to and was accepted at Boston University, Tulane University, Pepperdine University, Stanford University, the University of California at San Diego, Southern Methodist University, and Vanderbilt University. Several of these schools offered her financial aid.

It is undisputed that in the fall of 1991 Hope Calabro enrolled in and began attending Vanderbilt University with her father paying expenses that exceeded her scholarship. It is also undisputed that during the Christmas break of 1992 Arthur Calabro informed Hope Calabro that he was no longer willing to pay for her college expenses. Both parties agree that at that time he had prepaid her tuition for the spring of 1993 at Vanderbilt. It is undisputed that Plaintiff continued to attend Vanderbilt and completed her course work in the spring of 1995, earning a B.A. in psychology. What remains in dispute is whether Arthur Calabro formed a legally binding contract with his daughter to pay her college expenses and breached that contract by refusing to continue his support in December of 1992.

Plaintiff's complaint alleges that she moved to Nashville to attend Vanderbilt based upon defendant's representation that he would pay for all college tuition costs and living expenses in excess of plaintiff's scholarship while she was attending Vanderbilt. She avers that the defendant willfully repudiated his contract to pay all college tuition costs in excess of the scholarship that the plaintiff received, as well as all living expenses while she was attending Vanderbilt University. Plaintiff further alleges that due to his repudiation of the contract she financed these cost by taking out student loans that became due upon her graduation. Plaintiff demands compensatory damages representing the full extent of all college costs, including, but not limited to, outstanding student loans, personal living expenses during college, and other related expenses.

Defendant's answer admits that plaintiff attended Vanderbilt but denies that he made the representations as alleged in the complaint. Defendant admits that "he advised his daughter that if she entered and successfully remained in a course of study for the purpose of gaining admission to medical school, he would pay certain of her college related expenses while attending Vanderbilt University." He denies that plaintiff moved to Nashville and enrolled in Vanderbilt in response to his representation but admits that plaintiff enrolled in Vanderbilt and that she took out various student loans. He denies that he willfully repudiated his contract as alleged.

The trial court granted defendant summary judgment, and plaintiff has appealed, presenting three issues for review: (1) whether the trial court erred in holding that there was no valid consideration to support the defendant's promise of his offer to pay for his daughter's college expenses, (2) whether the court erred in holding that the contract between the parties was barred by the Statute of Frauds, and (3) whether the court erred in failing to enforce the defendant's promise under the doctrine of promissory estoppel. The trial court's order granting summary judgment did not state the reason therefor, and there is no transcript of the hearing on the motion for summary judgment to indicate that the trial judge made any such ruling from the bench. We perceive the dispositive issue to be whether the trial court erred in granting defendant's motion for summary judgment and will consider the arguments of counsel encompassed in the above-stated three issues.

A motion for summary judgment should be granted when the movant demonstrates that there are no genuine issues of material fact and that the moving party is entitled to a judgment as a matter of law. The party moving for summary judgment bears the burden of demonstrating that no genuine issue of material fact exists. On a motion for summary judgment, the court must take the strongest legitimate view of the evidence in favor of the nonmoving party, allow all reasonable inferences in favor of that party, and discard all countervailing evidence. In *Byrd v. Hall,* 847 S.W.2d 208 (Tenn.1993), our Supreme Court stated:

> Once it is shown by the moving party that there is no genuine issue of material fact, the nonmoving party must then demonstrate, by affidavits or discovery materials, that there is a genuine, material fact dispute to warrant a trial. In this regard, Rule 56.05 provides that the nonmoving party cannot simply rely upon his pleadings but must set forth *specific facts* showing that there is a genuine issue of material fact for trial.

Id. at 211 (citations omitted) (emphasis in original).

Summary judgment is only appropriate when the facts and the legal conclusions drawn from the facts reasonably permit only one conclusion. If the facts are uncontroverted, summary judgment is inappropriate if reasonable minds could differ as to the inferences to be drawn therefrom. Since only questions of law are involved, there is no presumption of correctness regarding a trial court's grant of summary judgment. Therefore, our review of the trial court's grant of summary judgment is *de novo* on the record before this Court.

Plaintiff contends that there was a binding contract between the parties and that defendant breached the contract when he refused to continue paying for her college expenses. Plaintiff contends that she undertook to do something that she was not legally obligated to do, thereby providing the consideration needed to form a contract. She asserts that defendant received a benefit by having his daughter close to him and away from her mother's influence, and by having a well-educated daughter. Plaintiff further asserts that she gave up substantial scholarships and financial aid at the University of Oklahoma, Tulane, Southern Methodist University, and Pepperdine to attend Vanderbilt. Plaintiff asserts that these foregone opportunities, along with the substantial expense she incurred to attend Vanderbilt, constitute a legal detriment to her as promisee and consideration for her father's promise to pay her education expenses.

Plaintiff asserts that the Statute of Frauds presents no bar to the enforcement of defendant's oral promise to pay his daughter's college expenses. Plaintiff contends that at the very least she partially performed the contract and thus comes within the exception of the Statute of Frauds. She asserts that actually she has fully performed the unilateral contract by attending and graduating from Vanderbilt University. Furthermore plaintiff contends that the doctrine of promissory estoppel takes the contract out of the Statute of Frauds because she detrimentally relied on her father's promise.

Defendant contends that the trial court properly determined that he was entitled to summary judgment as to his daughter's claim relating to expenses and debt incurred after May 1993 because there is no genuine issue of any material fact. He asserts that as a parent he has no legal obligation to pay for the educational expenses of a child that has reached the age of majority. Arthur Calabro asserts that he did not intend to enter into a contract that legally obligated him to pay for college expenses, but merely desired to help his daughter realize the dream she expressed to him of becoming a doctor. He further contends that even if his generosity could be construed as an obligation, it is a moral rather than a legal obligation, which is not legally enforceable. He asserts that his daughter's college attendance was not a benefit to him and that his satisfaction at having Hope attend school near his home was not an inducement, because he made no such requirement. Defendant maintains that the cause of any detriment to Hope was her failure to excel in school, and he, in fact, suffered the detriment of the expense of two years of his daughter's education.

Finally defendant asserts that in December of 1992, he made it clear to his daughter that he would pay no more after May, 1993, and it was not reasonable, necessary or justifiable for Hope to return to Vanderbilt and rely on further financial support based on his gratuitous promise.

"A contract has been defined over the years as an agreement, upon sufficient consideration, to do or not to do a particular thing." A party attempting to prove the existence of a contract "is required to show that the agreement on which he relies was supported by adequate consideration..." "[I]n all simple contracts ... whether written or verbal, the consideration must be averred and proved."

The question of what constitutes consideration adequate or sufficient to support a contract has been addressed by a number of Tennessee courts. The court in *University of Chattanooga v. Stansberry*, 9 Tenn.App. 341, 343 (1928) defined consideration as "either a benefit to the maker of the promise or a detriment to, or obligation upon the promise." (citing *Foust v. Board of Education*, 76 Tenn., (8 Lea), 552). Courts have been willing to find a contract based on facts from which a jury could infer the requisite consideration.

> For there to be a consideration in a contract between parties to the contract it is not necessary that something concrete and tangible move from one to the other. Any benefit to one and detriment to the other may be a sufficient consideration. The jury may draw any reasonable and natural inference from the proof and if by inference from the proof a benefit to the promisor and detriment to the promisee might be inferred this will constitute a valid consideration.

Palmer v. Dehn, 29 Tenn.App. 597, 599, 198 S.W.2d 827, 828 (1946); *see also Trailer Conditioners, Inc. v. Huddleston*, 897 S.W.2d 728, 731 (Tenn.App.1995); *Robinson v. Kenney*, 526 S.W.2d 115, 118–19 (Tenn.App.1973).

. . .

Simply stated, plaintiff's evidence from her deposition testimony, and the deposition of Mr. Calabro's sister[7], is that Mr. Calabro promised to pay her tuition and expenses over and above the $10,000.00 scholarship

---

[7] Mr. Calabro's sister testified that Mr. Calabro desired that his daughter attend Vanderbilt in order to be away from the influence of her mother and to be closer to him and thus strengthen the ties between father and daughter.

if she attended Vanderbilt. Plaintiff had previously been entitled to various scholarship opportunities at other colleges, but she relinquished those opportunities based upon the strength of defendant's promise. Although she preferred to go to another college, she deferred to Mr. Calabro's preference that she attend Vanderbilt. There was no condition attached to the promise to pay tuition that she maintain any sort of grade-point average or class standing, nor that she pursue any particular curriculum.

Defendant's testimony by deposition indicates that he did agree to pay the tuition and other expenses, but that he did not require that his daughter attend Vanderbilt. He admits that there was no condition attached that she pursue a pre-med curriculum or maintain a certain grade-point average.

We believe under the proof in this case that there is sufficient evidence to create a genuine issue of material fact as to whether there was adequate consideration flowing between the parties to constitute an enforceable contract. There is a dispute as to whether a benefit was conferred on defendant on his promise to pay the tuition and whether plaintiff suffered a detriment in her performance of the contract or agreement.

Defendant asserts that even if there was adequate consideration, the oral contract would be barred by the Statute of Frauds, T.C.A. § 29–2–101(a)(5)(1998), which provides:

> [U]pon any agreement or contract which is not to be performed within the space of one (1) year from the making of the agreement or contact; unless the promise or agreement, upon which such action shall be brought, or some memorandum or note thereof, shall be in writing, and signed by the party to be charged therewith, or some other person lawfully authorized by such party.

Plaintiff relies on her performance of the contract as excepting the contract from the operation of the statute.

The doctrine of part performance was utilized by the court in *Blasingame v. American Materials, Inc.,* 654 S.W.2d 659 (Tenn.1983) in enforcing an oral contract where over a period of years, the

> plaintiff was led to believe that the oral employment contract he made with defendant corporation would be honored; that in reliance thereon, plaintiff proceeded to perform his part of the bargain; and that in doing so, he so altered his position as to suffer an unconscionable loss if the corporation was allowed to rely on the Statue of Frauds. There is material

evidence in this record to support those concurrent factual findings and they are binding on this Court.

Id. at 663. The Supreme Court found that such facts brought the plaintiff within the exception of part performance, and the plaintiff thereby avoided the Statute of Frauds. *Id.*

. . .

Plaintiff also relies upon the doctrine of promissory estoppel as an exception to the Statute of Frauds. Promissory estoppel is explained as:

A promise which the promisor should reasonably expect to induce action or forbearance on the part of the promisee or a third person and which does induce such action or forbearance is binding if injustice can be avoided only by enforcement of the promise. The remedy granted for breach may be limited as justice requires.

Amacher v. Brown–Forman Corp., 826 S.W.2d 480, 482 (Tenn.App.1991) (quoting *Restatement (Second) of Contracts* § 90); *see also Alden v. Presley* 637 S.W.2d 862, 864 (Tenn.1982).

There are limits to the application of promissory estoppel:

Detrimental action or forbearance by the promisee in reliance on a gratuitous promise, within limits constitutes a substitute for consideration, or a sufficient reason for enforcement of the promise without consideration. This doctrine is known as promissory estoppel. A promisor who induces substantial change of position by the promisee in reliance on the promise is estopped to deny its enforceability as lacking consideration. The reason for the doctrine is to avoid an unjust result, and its reason defines its limits. No injustice results in refusal to enforce a gratuitous promise where the loss suffered in reliance is negligible, nor where the promisee's action in reliance was unreasonable or unjustified by the promise. The limits of promissory estoppel are: (1) the detriment suffered in reliance must be substantial in an economic sense; (2) the substantial loss to the promisee in acting in reliance must have been foreseeable by the promisor; (3) the promisee must have acted reasonable in justifiable reliance on the promise as made.

Alden 637 S.W.2d at 864 (citing L. Simpson, Law of Contracts § 61 (2d ed.1965)).

The doctrine of promissory estoppel is also referred to as "detrimental reliance" because the plaintiff must show not only that a promise was made, but also that the plaintiff reasonably relied on the promise to his detriment. Furthermore the promise upon which the promisee relied must be unambiguous and not unenforceably vague. However, a "claim of promissory estoppel is not dependent upon the existence of an expressed contract between the parties". . . .

From our review of the record, we conclude that there are disputes of material fact as to the alleged promises of defendant, the plaintiff's action and response thereto, and any inferences that legitimately may be drawn therefrom. The trier of fact should first determine whether a valid contract exists between the parties. In this regard, our Supreme Court stated in *Johnson v. Central Nat'l Ins. Co.,* 210 Tenn. 24, 356 S.W.2d 277 (1962):

> While a contract may be either expressed or implied, or written or oral, it must result from a meeting of the minds of the parties in mutual assent to the terms, must be based upon a sufficient consideration, free from fraud or undue influence, not against public policy and sufficiently definite to be enforced. *American Lead Pencil Company v. Nashville, Chattanooga & St. Louis Ry. Co.,* 124 Tenn. 57, 134 S.W. 613, 32 L.R.A., N.S., 323.

Id. at 281.

Alternatively, the trier of fact should determine whether plaintiff may rely upon the theory of promissory estoppel.

Accordingly, the order of the trial court granting summary judgment is reversed and this case is remanded for such further proceedings as necessary. Costs of appeal are assessed to appellee.

NOTES AND QUESTIONS

1. What do you think? If you were the judge in this case, what would you do? Do you think the elements for a valid, enforceable contract were present in this case? Would you enforce this promise with legal sanctions, or would you conclude that this type of promise is best handled by some other institution or government such as the family or the church?

_____

_____

_____

    2. Promissory Estoppel.   Promissory estoppel or detrimental reliance is a concept that is used to enforce a promise upon which someone has detrimentally relied, even when, for some reason or another, the elements for a valid, enforceable contract are not present. What elements were possibly missing or what defense could possibly have been raised in this case that would make promissory estoppel necessary for Hope to get the assistance of the civil magistrate in enforcing this promise?

    That said, is promissory estoppel consistent with the Christian worldview of contracts discussed earlier? In other words, if the elements for a valid, enforceable contract are not met, should the civil magistrate always refuse to act? What do you think justice demands? *See Exodus* 23:1-9; *Leviticus* 19:15; and *Deuteronomy* 1:16-17.

    After you have considered these questions for yourself, read Prof. Bern's analysis of a similar hypothetical at Roger Bern, *Biblical Model, supra*, at 136-138. Do you agree or disagree with Prof. Bern's analysis?

_____

_____

_____

_____

_____

    3. Other Christian Worldview Issues in the Contracts Setting. Obviously, the role of the civil magistrate is a very important consideration in contracts law. You will also see other important Christian worldview issues or principles as you study contracts law including the sanctity of the promise, the voluntariness of committing oneself to a promise, and the importance of the right to and freedom of contract to economic liberty.

CHAPTER 2
ECONOMIC LIBERTY AND THE RIGHT TO CONTRACT

In the previous chapter, we considered the very important issue of the role of the civil magistrate in enforcing contracts. In order to do this, we considered the question "what is a contract?" We saw that this led us to a consideration of the elements of a valid, enforceable contract as a means of determining when a promise or set of promises rises to the level of a contract and therefore is subject to enforcement by the civil magistrate with legal sanctions.

Further, at the end of the chapter, we saw that there are other important Christian worldview principles and issues that arise in contracts law. One such issue is the sanctity or sacredness of the promise. God views vows very seriously and does not suffer liars. *See, e.g., Numbers* 30:2, *Deuteronomy* 23:21, and *Ecclesiastes* 5:1-7. Accordingly, we should expect the legal system to have a very high view of the sacredness of promises. Another such issue is the voluntariness of contracts. God does not require that we make many vows, but, when we do make them, He expects us to fulfill them. Accordingly, an important Christian worldview issue in contracts law is voluntariness. Several elements, such as agreement and consideration address this from various angles.

And, lastly, a very important issue in contracts law is the freedom of or the right to contract. This is a liberty issue, and it builds on the idea of the origin of rights discussed in the previous chapter. Rights derive from our duties to God. We have a duty to use everything that God has given us—time, treasure, talents, etc.—for His glory. As we have seen previously, this can be referred to as the stewardship-dominion mandate or duties. Thus, based upon this duty that we owe God, we have a right to be free from the interference of others (other individuals, the family, the church, and the civil government) in the discharge of this duty. This gives rise to a particular type of liberty that is often overlooked in our time; I will refer to it herein as economic liberty, i.e., the right to use the resources that God has entrusted me in the manner I see fit.

In this regard, it can be said that there are three broad categories of liberty: political liberty, religious liberty, and economic liberty. All three are very important, and one people enjoying all three at the same time is almost unheard of in history. In fact, it can be argued that the first (and only) time it ever occurred in the history of the world was at the era of the American founding.

At the time of the founding of America, the governmental system created by the Constitution and the various state and local governments served to diffuse the power of the civil government and limit it, to a large degree, to its proper biblical role or jurisdiction, as discussed to some degree in the previous chapter. As the power of the civil magistrate (and particularly the federal or central government) has grown in America, these important liberties have been steadily eroded as the civil magistrate has grown beyond its God-given limitations. Indeed, the Constitutional Republic of the founding era hardly exists today, having been replaced with something much closer to a European-style socialist democracy than the carefully limited civil government envisioned by our nation's founders.

It is not discussed as often as the other liberties, but the Founders clearly believed that economic liberty was a very important God-given liberty. In fact, it is entirely possible that the phrase "the pursuit of happiness" used in the Declaration of Independence is a reference to the right to private property and economic liberty. This very important Christian worldview principle arises in contract law in the context of the freedom of or right to contract.

In order to protect the important right to fulfill our stewardship-dominion duties to God, the civil magistrate should have a disposition toward allowing people to have the freedom to or right to contract as they see fit and toward enforcing these contracts that people make without inquiry into the substance of the deal or forcing terms into the deal. Without being able to enter into contracts and seek their enforcement when they are breached, it becomes very difficult to engage in the type of economic activity that would allow us to glorify God with what He has entrusted to us. *See, e.g., Matthew* 25:14-30 and *Luke* 19:21-27. Thus, it becomes obvious that the right to contract, and the corollary right to have those contracts enforced according to the terms that the parties agreed to, is an essential component to economic liberty.[1]

However, as noted earlier, our liberties in America have been steadily eroded since the founding era. In fact, a strong argument could be made that our economic liberties have actually been eroded even more than the other liberties. Many examples abound, and we will have an opportunity to look at some of them throughout this course. An example that is very much in the minds of many Americas at the time of the writing of this chapter is the healthcare reform act known as Obamacare. It requires that every American purchase a product—health insurance— or pay a penalty (or tax?).[2] That is an astounding encroachment by the civil magistrate onto our economic liberties.

As we shall see throughout the course, many of the encroachments on the freedom of contract and economic liberty are not so blatant and "in-your-face" as Obamacare. On the contrary, throughout our nation's history, they have often been more subtle, couched in terms of regulations and restrictions that many Americas hardly even know about.

The milk industry in America is a case in point. It is subject to an astounding array of regulations and controls such that economic freedom and the freedom to contract has been all but eliminated (and many Americans don't even know about these regulations and controls.) For example, the simple act of a farmer selling milk fresh from his cow is illegal in many states and regulated to some degree in all states. In other words and by way of illustration, in the Commonwealth of Virginia, where I live, it is illegal for me to contract to purchase a gallon of milk with a neighbor who owns a dairy cow and would very much like to sell me milk from said cow (unless, of course, he is willing to spend thousands of dollars to pasteurize the milk and comply with a bevy of other federal and state regulations.)[3]

---

[1] *See, e.g.,* Roger Bern, *A Biblical Model for Analysis of Issues of Law and Public Policy: with Illustrative Applications to Contracts, Antitrust, Remedies and Public Policy Issues,* 6 Regent U. L. Rev. 103, 131-153 (1995), and Herbert W. Titus, *God, Man, and Law: The Biblical Principles* 219-223 (1994). On the goodness of commercial activity in general, *see* Rodney D. Chrisman, *Can a Merchant Please God?: The Church's Historic Teaching on the Goodness of Just Commercial Activity as a Foundational Principle of Commercial Law Jurisprudence,* 6 Liberty U. L. Rev. 453 (2012) and Wayne Grudem, *Business for the Glory of God: The Bible's Teaching on the Moral Goodness of Business* (2003).

[2] *National Federation of Independent Businesses v. Sebelius,* ____ U.S. _____, 132 S.Ct. 2566 (2012) (upholding Obamacare as Constitutional in a very split and arguably irrational opinion).

[3] *See, e.g.,* Joel Salatin, *Everything I Want to do is Illegal: War Stories from the Local Food Front* 12-26 (2007) and Ron Schmid, *The Untold Story of Milk: the History, Politics, and Science of Nature's Perfect Food: Raw Milk from Pasture-Fed Cows* (2005).

However, not only is it illegal for me to purchase milk from my neighbor the farmer, as the following case demonstrates, the price I pay for milk at the grocery store is also largely controlled by the civil magistrate. As you read the case, consider how greatly economic liberty and the concomitant freedom of contract has been eroded in the past century or so.

Hettinga v. United States
677 F.3d 471 (D.C. Cir. 2012)

PER CURIAM:

Plaintiff-appellants Hein and Ellen Hettinga appeal the dismissal of their constitutional challenges to two provisions of the Milk Regulatory Equity Act of 2005 ("MREA"). The Hettingas alleged that the provisions, which subjected certain large producer-handlers of milk to contribution requirements applicable to all milk handlers, constituted a bill of attainder and violated the Equal Protection and Due Process Clauses. The district court disagreed, and we affirm.

I

Milk markets in the United States are regulated by a complex system of price controls dating back to the New Deal. The Agricultural Marketing Agreement Act of 1937, ("AMAA"), authorizes the Secretary of Agriculture to issue regional milk marketing orders that govern payments from milk processors and distributors ("handlers") to dairy farmers ("producers"). *Id.* Under a typical milk market order, a dairy farmer supplies raw milk to a processor or distributor, and the handler pays money into a centralized "producer settlement fund" at fixed prices based on the intended use of the milk. Handlers using their milk for "high value" uses, such as fluid milk, pay higher prices than handlers that engage in "low-value" uses, such as the processing of butter or cheese. The money that handlers pay into the producer settlement fund is then proportionally redistributed to milk producers at a uniform "blend price" based on quantity of milk sold. This system ensures that all dairy farmers receive the same price for their raw milk regardless of whether they sell to high-value or low-value handlers.

Firms that operate as both producers and handlers create serious complications for this system. In such cases, there is no opportunity for the producer-handler to pay into the centralized producer settlement fund because there is no intermediate sale of raw milk. Until recently, the

Secretary of Agriculture therefore exempted producer-handlers from the pricing and pooling requirements of federal milk marketing orders. The pricing and pooling requirements also did not apply to handlers who sold milk in geographic areas that were not regulated by federal milk marketing orders, even if the handler itself was located in a federally-regulated area.

The Hettingas own two dairy operations that fell within these exemptions. The first is Sarah Farms, an integrated producer-handler located in Yuma, Arizona. Sarah Farms processes and sells over three million pounds of its own milk per month in the federally regulated Arizona Marketing Area. The second is GH Dairy, an independent milk processing plant which they own in partnership with their son. GH Dairy, a handler located in Arizona, processes raw milk into bottled milk and milk products that are sold exclusively in California. Because California is not a federally regulated milk marketing area, GH Dairy was not subject to the federal pricing and pooling requirements.

On February 24, 2006, the USDA adopted a Final Rule that would have eliminated the producer-handler exemption for firms that operate in the Arizona and Pacific Northwest Marketing Areas and sell more than three million pounds of their own milk per month—a group that includes Sarah Farms. *See Milk in the Pacific Northwest and Arizona–Las Vegas Marketing Areas; Order Amending the Orders,* 71 Fed.Reg. 9,430 (Feb. 24, 2006) ("USDA Rule"). The decision to eliminate the exemption for these large producer-handlers was based on evidence of "disorderly marketing conditions"—specifically, that large producer-handlers were obtaining a "competitive sales advantage" over fully-regulated handlers, and were causing a "measurabl[e] and significant[ ]" decrease in the blend price being paid to regulated producers. *Milk in the Pacific Northwest and Arizona–Las Vegas Marketing Areas; Final Decision on Proposed Amendments to Marketing Agreement and to Orders,* 70 Fed.Reg. 74,166, 74,186–88 (Dec. 14, 2005). The USDA Rule was scheduled to go into effect on April 1, 2006. The Hettingas filed suit in the U.S. District Court for the Northern District of Texas, challenging the legality of the USDA Rule and seeking a preliminary injunction Oral argument was scheduled for March 29, 2006.

On the day before the Texas district court heard arguments in the Hettingas' case, Congress amended the AMAA by passing the MREA. President Bush subsequently signed the MREA into law on April 11, 2006. Subsection N of the MREA, 7 U.S.C. § 608c(5)(N), codified the USDA Rule's revocation of the exemption for large producer-handlers in the Arizona Marketing Area, including Sarah Farms. Unlike the USDA Rule, however, it applied neither to Nevada, which Congress exempted from coverage by any federal milk marketing orders, nor to the Pacific Northwest Milk Marketing Area. Subsection M of the MREA, *id.* §

608c(5)(M), imposed the federal pricing and pooling requirements on handlers, like GH Dairy, that were located in a federally regulated area but sold packaged milk exclusively in a state not covered by a federal milk marketing order, such as California.

The Hettingas challenged the constitutionality of the MREA in the U.S. District Court for the District of Columbia. First, they alleged that Subsections M and N of the MREA violate the Bill of Attainder Clause by singling them out for legislative punishment. Compl. ¶¶ 53–57. Second, the Hettingas claim the MREA denies them equal protection by "singling them out for adverse treatment that is extended to no other producer-handler in any other Milk Marketing Area." *Id.* ¶ 65. Finally, they claim the MREA denied them due process of law by foreclosing judicial review of the USDA Rule in the Northern District of Texas. *Id.* ¶ 60. The district court initially dismissed the Hettingas' claims for failure to exhaust administrative remedies, but this Court reversed and remanded, holding that the AMAA's exhaustion requirements do not apply to facial constitutional challenges. *Hettinga v. United States,* 560 F.3d 498, 504–06 (D.C.Cir.2009). On remand, the district court dismissed the Hettingas' complaint for failure to state a claim under Fed.R.Civ.P. 12(b)(6) and denied leave to file a supplemental complaint. *Hettinga v. United States,* 770 F.Supp.2d 51 (D.D.C.2011).

. . .

II

[In this section of the opinion, based upon prior Supreme Court precedent, the court denied the Hettingas' argument that the MREA amounts to a bill of attainder because it applies only to them.]

III

We grant statutes involving economic policy a "strong presumption of validity." *FCC v. Beach Commc'ns, Inc.,* 508 U.S. 307, 314, 113 S.Ct. 2096, 124 L.Ed.2d 211 (1993). A statutory classification that "neither proceeds along suspect lines nor infringes fundamental constitutional rights must be upheld against equal protection challenge if there is any reasonably conceivable state of facts that could provide a rational basis for the classification." *Id.* at 313, 113 S.Ct. 2096. "Where there are plausible reasons for Congress' action, our inquiry is at an end." *Id.* at 313–14, 113 S.Ct. 2096. The challenger bears the burden of showing that the statute is not a rational means of advancing a legitimate government purpose. *See Bd. of Trs. of the Univ. of Ala. v. Garrett,* 531 U.S. 356, 367, 121 S.Ct. 955, 148 L.Ed.2d 866 (2001).

The district court dismissed the Hettingas' equal protection claim because it found the MREA provides a rational means of ensuring orderly milk markets by (1) preventing handlers located in regulated regions from gaining advantages over their competitors by exporting milk to unregulated regions and (2) preventing large producer-handlers in a federally-regulated region from undercutting other handlers in that region with unregulated sales. On appeal, the Hettingas claim the district court applied too deferential a standard of review, arguing that rational basis review is "not [ ] toothless." *Logan v. Zimmerman Brush Co.,* 455 U.S. 422, 439, 102 S.Ct. 1148, 71 L.Ed.2d 265 (1982) (Blackmun, J., concurring).

Regardless of how Justice Blackmun characterized rational basis review, the Supreme Court's subsequent decision in *Beach* makes clear that "not toothless" does not mean "growling." Here, the government provided a rational explanation for its decision to close two loopholes in the AMAA scheme—that large dairy businesses have used the exemptions to gain a substantial—and ultimately disruptive—competitive advantage over their regulated competitors. *Beach* requires us to accept this explanation and end our inquiry here. *See Beach Commc'ns,* 508 U.S. at 313–14, 113 S.Ct. 2096. Although the classification might indeed be unfair to the Hettingas, mere disparity of treatment is not sufficient to state an equal protection violation.

. . .

For the foregoing reasons, the decision of the district court is

Affirmed.

BROWN, Circuit Judge, with whom Chief Judge SENTELLE joins, concurring:

I agree fully with the court's opinion. Given the long-standing precedents in this area no other result is possible. Our precedents forced the Hettingas to make a difficult legal argument. No doubt they would have preferred a simpler one—that the operation and production of their enterprises had been impermissibly collectivized—but a long line of constitutional adjudication precluded that claim.

The Hettingas' sense of ill-usage is understandable. So is their consternation at being confronted with the gap between the rhetoric of free markets and the reality of ubiquitous regulation. The Hettingas' collision with the MREA—the latest iteration of the venerable AMAA— reveals an ugly truth: America's cowboy capitalism was long ago disarmed by a democratic process increasingly dominated by powerful groups with economic interests antithetical to competitors and consumers. And the courts, from which the victims of burdensome regulation sought protection, have been negotiating the terms of surrender since the 1930s.

First the Supreme Court allowed state and local jurisdictions to regulate property, pursuant to their police powers, in the public interest, and to "adopt whatever economic policy may reasonably be deemed to promote public welfare." *Nebbia v. New York*, 291 U.S. 502, 516, 54 S.Ct. 505, 78 L.Ed. 940 (1934). Then the Court relegated economic liberty to a lower echelon of constitutional protection than personal or political liberty, according restrictions on property rights only minimal review. *United States v. Carolene Products Co.*, 304 U.S. 144, 152–53, 58 S.Ct. 778, 82 L.Ed. 1234 (1938). Finally, the Court abdicated its constitutional duty to protect economic rights completely, acknowledging that the only recourse for aggrieved property owners lies in the "democratic process." *Vance v. Bradley*, 440 U.S. 93, 97, 99 S.Ct. 939, 59 L.Ed.2d 171 (1979). "The Constitution," the Court said, "presumes that, absent some reason to infer antipathy, even improvident decisions will eventually be rectified by the democratic process and that judicial intervention is generally unwarranted no matter how unwisely we may think a political branch has acted." *Id.*

As the dissent predicted in *Nebbia*, the judiciary's refusal to consider the wisdom of legislative acts—at least to inquire whether its purpose and the means proposed are "within legislative power"—would lead to only one result: "[R]ights guaranteed by the Constitution [would] exist only so long as supposed public interest does not require their extinction." 291 U.S. at 523, 54 S.Ct. 505. In short order that baleful prophecy received the court's imprimatur. In *Carolene Products* (yet another case involving protectionist legislation), the court ratified minimalist review of economic regulations, holding that a rational basis for economic legislation would be presumed and more searching inquiry would be reserved for intrusions on political rights. 304 U.S. at 153 n. 4, 58 S.Ct. 778.

Thus the Supreme Court decided economic liberty was not a fundamental constitutional right, and decreed economic legislation must be upheld against an equal protection challenge "if there is any reasonably conceivable state of facts that could provide a rational basis" for it. *FCC v. Beach Commc'ns, Inc.*, 508 U.S. 307, 313, 113 S.Ct. 2096, 124 L.Ed.2d 211 (1993). *See also Pac. States Box & Basket Co. v. White*, 296 U.S. 176, 185–86, 56 S.Ct. 159, 80 L.Ed. 138 (1935); *Steffan v. Perry*, 41 F.3d 677, 684–85 (D.C.Cir.1994) (en banc).

This standard is particularly troubling in light of the pessimistic view of human nature that animated the Framing of the Constitution—a worldview that the American polity and its political handmaidens have, unfortunately, shown to be largely justified. *See* James Madison, *Notes of*

Debates in the Federal Convention of 1787, at 39, 42 (W.W. Norton & Co. 1987). Moreover, what the Framers theorized about the destructive potential of factions (now known as special or group interests), experience has also shown to be true. The Federalist No. 10, at 78, 81 (James Madison) (Clinton Rossiter ed., 1961). The judiciary has worried incessantly about the "countermajoritarian difficulty" when interpreting the Constitution. But the better view may be that the Constitution *created* the countermajoritarian difficulty in order to thwart more potent threats to the Republic: the political temptation to exploit the public appetite for other people's money—either by buying consent with broad-based entitlements or selling subsidies, licensing restrictions, tariffs, or price fixing regimes to benefit narrow special interests.

The Hettingas believe they are the victims of just such shenanigans. Compl. ¶¶ 40–45. And press accounts during the height of the controversy support the claim. *See* Dan Morgan, Sarah Cohen, & Gilbert M. Gaul, "Dairy Industry Crushed Innovator Who Bested Price–Control System," Wash. Post, Dec. 10, 2006, *available at* http://www.washingtonpost.com/wpdyn/content/article/2006/12/09/AR2006 120900925.html. The Washington Post described Hein Hettinga as an American success story. He emigrated to the U.S. after World War II and started as a hired hand. By 1990, Hettinga owned half a dozen dairies and decided to build his own bottling business. A Costco vice president showed reporters copies of an e-mail he sent to Senator Reid during the legislative debate, explaining that Southern California purchasers of milk were the victims of "a brazen case of price gouging and profiteering by the strongest, largest market suppliers," who turned a deaf ear to the company's call for lower prices. Hein Hettinga changed all that. His arrangement with Costco "lowered the average price of milk by 20 cents a gallon overnight" until two senators, one from each party, pushed through the milk legislation at issue in this case.

Very little seems to have changed since the Supreme Court's initial confrontation with the regulation of milk pricing in *Nebbia*. The state of New York, responding to falling prices caused by the Great Depression, created a Milk Control Board, which proposed to remedy weak demand by establishing a minimum price for milk, and making sale of milk at any lower price a crime. 291 U.S. at 515, 519, 54 S.Ct. 505. Leo Nebbia sold two quarts of milk and a five-cent loaf of bread for eighteen cents, and was convicted of violating the board's order. *Id.* at 515, 54 S.Ct. 505.

Even Justice McReynolds saw the irony. The law, he said, "impose[d] direct and arbitrary burdens upon those already seriously impoverished" to give special benefits to others. *Id.* at 557, 54 S.Ct. 505. "To him with less than 9 cents it says: You cannot procure a quart of milk from the grocer although he is anxious to accept what you can pay and the demands of your household are urgent! A superabundance; but no child can purchase from a willing storekeeper below the figure appointed by three men at headquarters!" *Id.* at 557–58, 54 S.Ct. 505.

    To be sure, the economic climate in which the New York legislature enacted the law at issue in *Nebbia* was truly dire, but 78 years later, the same tired trope about "disorderly market conduct" is still extant. The Hettingas built their business on an exemption—one that was profitable for them and beneficial for consumers. The government acknowledged that the decision to eliminate the exemption was based on evidence that large producer-handlers were obtaining a "decisive competitive advantage" over fully-regulated handlers, Appellees' Br. at 7, and were causing a measurable and "significant[ ]" decrease in the blend prices being paid to regulated handlers. *See* 70 Fed.Reg. 74,166, 74,186 (Dec. 14, 2005). As another court has noted, federal regulation of milk pricing "is premised on dissatisfaction with the results of competition." *Alto Dairy v. Veneman,* 336 F.3d 560, 562 (7th Cir.2003). "[M]ilk price discrimination is intended to redistribute wealth from consumers to producers of milk." *Id.* Once again, the government has thwarted the free market, and ultimately hurt consumers, to protect the economic interests of a powerful faction. Neither the legislators nor the lobbyists broke any positive laws to accomplish this result. It just *seems* like a crime.

    The judiciary justifies its reluctance to intervene by claiming incompetence—apparently, judges lack the acumen to recognize corruption, self-interest, or arbitrariness in the economic realm—or deferring to the majoritarian imperative. *But see* The Federalist No. 78, at 467 (Alexander Hamilton) (Clinton Rossiter ed., 1961). The practical effect of rational basis review of economic regulation is the absence of any check on the group interests that all too often control the democratic process. It allows the legislature free rein to subjugate the common good and individual liberty to the electoral calculus of politicians, the whim of majorities, or the self-interest of factions. *See* Randy E. Barnett, Restoring the Lost Constitution: The Presumption of Liberty 260 (2004).

    The hope of correction at the ballot box is purely illusory. *See generally* Ilya Somin, *Political Ignorance and the Counter–Majoritarian Difficulty: A New Perspective on the Central Obsession of Constitutional Theory,* 89 Iowa L.Rev. 1287 (2004). In an earlier century, H.L. Mencken offered a blunt assessment of that option: "[G]overnment is a broker in pillage, and every election is a sort of advance auction sale of stolen goods." On Politics: A Carnival of Buncombe 331 (1996). And, as the Hettingas can attest, it's no good hoping the process will heal itself. Civil society, "once it grows addicted to redistribution, changes its character and comes to require the state to 'feed its habit.'" Anthony De Jasay, The State 226 (1998). The difficulty of assessing net benefits and burdens makes the idea of public choice oxymoronic. *See id.* at 248. Rational basis review means property is at the mercy of the pillagers. The constitutional guarantee of liberty deserves more respect—a lot more.

GRIFFITH, Circuit Judge, concurring:

I, too, agree fully with the per curiam opinion, but do not join my colleagues' concurrence with its spirited criticism of the Supreme Court's long-standing approach to claims of economic liberty. Although by no means unsympathetic to their criticism nor critical of their choice to express their perspective, I am reluctant to set forth my own views on the wisdom of such a broad area of the Supreme Court's settled jurisprudence that was not challenged by the petitioner.

NOTES AND QUESTIONS

1. Got Milk? As this case demonstrates, there is much more behind buying that gallon of milk at the grocery store than most of us realize. Prior to reading this, did you know the extent of the regulations and control on the milk industry in America? Does it surprise you? Do you think most Americas know and understand all of this? (And, of course, milk is just one example. Many other areas of the economy, from employment relationships to other agricultural products to airlines to securities, are heavily regulated with the government dictating many, if not most, of the terms of the contracts in these areas.)

Is there something unjust about just the very fact alone that all of this is so complicated and secret? Obviously, it can be found out, but, while the milk industry very much wants you to ask the question "got milk?", they do not want you to consider how you got it. (Or, as my dad used to say, "if it's good, I don't see why it has to be so secret.")

_____

_____

_____

_____

_____

_____

2. The Erosion of Economic Liberty. Can you explain how regulations and controls such as those described in this case erode our economic liberty? In explaining this, perhaps it would help you to consider some additional questions.

Who benefits from regulations and controls such as these? Consumers? Producers? Farmers? Big companies or small companies or family farms? Review the dissenting opinion above. What do the dissenting judges think?

What is the proper role of the government here? Do these regulations and controls fit within punishing evildoers? Or, do they simply work to transfer wealth from one group to another as the dissent suggestions? If so, where does transferring wealth fit within the biblical role of the civil magistrate described in chapter 1?

How do you think such as system is justified to the public when it is discussed? Are you persuaded by these justifications?

Do these regulations make it easier or harder for competitors to enter the milk market? If you felt called to go into small-scale, natural dairy farming, would these regulations make it harder or easier for you to do that? Why should the government dictate the terms of the contracts that you would enter into if you want to sell the milk and your neighbors want to buy it?

---

3. The Most Lenient Standard of Review. The Supreme Court uses different tests in reviewing government actions to consider whether they violate rights guaranteed by the Constitution. Some of these tests are very, very demanding, and very few laws survive analysis under these tests (for example, strict scrutiny analysis.) However, for economic liberty issues, the Supreme Court has adopted the most lenient standard of review—rational basis. This reflects a view that economic liberty is not as important as other types of liberty. Do you agree with the Supreme Court? Or, are you persuaded by the dissenting opinion in *Hettinga*?

CHAPTER 3
THE ORIGIN OF THE RIGHT TO CONTRACT

An important Christian worldview principle in the law of contracts is that promises are sacred. Since promises are sacred, certain types of promises are subject to enforcement by the civil magistrate. The importance of the sanctity of promises in society should lead us naturally to ask from where does this sacredness or sanctity come?

In the following famous case, Chief Justice John Marshall discusses the issue of the origins of contract law. Specifically, he is addressing whether the right to enter into contracts and have them enforced comes from the civil government or from the way God made things. While the language is older and can therefore be difficult, it is worth the effort. (To aid you in this worthy endeavor, I have used a number of footnotes in this opinion to offer some commentary on Justice Marshall's text modeled something after the way commentators use footnotes to explain and expound upon the biblical text in a study Bible.)

Justice Marshall was a fantastic leader on the Supreme Court who shaped early American law. He was gifted at bringing people over to his way of thinking, and during his long years on the court he wrote only a handful a dissenting opinions (in other words, he was almost always in the majority.) However, he felt the issues in the following case, one of which is the origin of contracts, to be so important that he dissented to set forth his views. As you read the opinion, consider where the right to enter into contracts and have them enforced comes from—the civil government or the Creator God? Also, consider why Justice Marshall thought the answer to this question to be so important.

Ogden v. Saunders
25 U.S. 213, 344-57 (1827)

Mr. Chief Justice MARSHALL [writing in dissent for himself and Justices
Duvall and Story]

. . .

Contract, it is said, being the creature of society, derives its
obligation from the law; and, although the law may not enter into the
agreement so as to form a constituent part of it, still it acts externally
upon the contract, and determines how far the principle of coercion shall
be applied to it; and this being universally understood, no individual can
complain justly of its application to himself, in a case where it was known
when the contract was formed.

. . .

The defendants maintain that an error lies at the very foundation
of this argument. It assumes that contract is the mere creature of society,
and derives all its obligation from human legislation. That it is not the
stipulation an individual makes which binds him, but some declaration of
the supreme power of a State to which he belongs, that he shall perform
what he has undertaken to perform. That though this original declaration
may be lost in remote antiquity, it must be presumed as the origin of the
obligation of contracts. This postulate the defendants deny, and, we think,
with great reason.[1]

It is an argument of no inconsiderable weight against it, that we
find no trace of such an enactment. So far back as human research carries
us, we find the judicial power as a part of the executive, administering
justice by the application of remedies to violated rights, or broken
contracts. We find that power applying these remedies on the idea of a
pre-existing obligation on every man to do what he has promised on
consideration to do; that the breach of this obligation is an injury for
which the injured party has a just claim to compensation, and that society
ought to afford him a remedy for that injury. We find allusions to the

---

[1] Editor's Note: Justice Marshall is here noting that the argument forwarded by
the defendants and to some measure adopted by the majority opinion is that contract law
is essentially positive law only, i.e., it derives it origin, support, and power from the state
or the civil magistrate, or, as Justice Marshall puts it, society. This is as opposed to
contract law finding its origin, support, and power in the law of nature and nature's God,
to borrow a phrase from the Declaration of Independence. Justice Marshall believes it to
be the later and not the former, as the opinion makes clear.

mode of acquiring property, but we find no allusion, from the earliest time, to any supposed act of the governing power giving obligation to contracts. On the contrary, the proceedings respecting them of which we know any thing, evince the idea of a pre-existing intrinsic obligation which human law enforces. If, on tracing the right to contract, and the obligations created by contract, to their source, we find them to exist anterior to, and independent of society, we may reasonably conclude that those original and pre-existing principles are, like many other natural rights, brought with man into society; and, although they may be controlled, are not given by human legislation.[2]

In the rudest state of nature[3] a man governs himself, and labours for his own purposes. That which he acquires is his own, at least while in his possession, and he may transfer it to another. This transfer passes his right to that other. Hence the right to barter. One man may have acquired more skins than are necessary for his protection from the cold; another more food than is necessary for his immediate use. They agree each to supply the wants of the other from his surplus. Is this contract without obligation? If one of them, having received and eaten the food he needed, refuses to deliver the skin, may not the other rightfully compel him to deliver it? Or two persons agree to unite their strength and skill to hunt together for their mutual advantage, engaging to divide the animal they shall master. Can one of them rightfully take the whole? or, should

---

[2] Editor's Note: In other words, the United States federal government nor the government of the Commonwealth of Virginia endow me with the right to enter into contracts. Rather, Marshall argues, that right is mine inherently. Again, to borrow a phrase from the Declaration of Independence, we might say that I have been endowed by my Creator with certain inalienable rights, among which is the right to bind myself to contracts and to seek to have contracts to which I am a party enforced.

[3] Editor's Note: Justice Marshall is here referring to a simpler state of affairs and societal organization where there is little or no functioning civil government. For example, in the book of *Genesis* in the Bible, there is very little civil government to which the patriarchs are subject prior to entering Egypt. Abraham, Isaac, and Jacob appear largely to have been governed by self-government and family government, and, while they interacted with certain civil governments (such as Abimelech of the Philistines,) they appeared to be only loosely subject to such governments. *See, e.g., Genesis* 13 (Abraham and Lot enter into an agreement to separate that both assumed would be binding), 21:22-34 (Abraham and Abimelech, a Philistine ruler, enter into a treaty), 23 (Abraham enters into a contract to purchase the field in Machpelah from Ephron as a burial place for Sarah), 25:29-24 (Esau enters into an agreement with Jacob to transfer Jacob his birthright in exchange for some stew), 26:6-33 (Isaac and Abimelech enter into an agreement similar to the one that Abraham entered into with the Philistines), and 28-31 (Jacob enters into a series of agreements with Laban). (It is worthy to note that, in many of these early "contracts," it appears that the only authority that could be called upon to enforce them was the Lord Himself, presumably because there was no civil magistrate to which all parties were subject.) Accordingly, by looking at this "rudest state of nature" and finding binding contracts, Justice Marshall is going to make the argument that the right to contract therefore precedes organized civil "society" and therefore inures in the nature of mankind.

he attempt it, may not the other force him to a division? If the answer to these questions must affirm the duty of keeping faith between these parties, and the right to enforce it if violated, the answer admits the obligation of contracts, because, upon that obligation depends the right to enforce them. Superior strength may give the power, but cannot give the right. The rightfulness of coercion must depend on the pre-existing obligation to do that for which compulsion is used.[4] It is no objection to the principle, that the injured party may be the weakest. In society, the wrong-doer may be too powerful for the law. He may deride its coercive power, yet his contracts are obligatory; and, if society acquire the power of coercion, that power will be applied without previously enacting that his contract is obligatory.

Independent nations are individuals in a state of nature. Whence is derived the obligation of their contracts? They admit the existence of no superior legislative power which is to give them validity, yet their validity is acknowledged by all. If one of these contracts be broken, all admit the right of the injured party to demand reparation for the injury, and to enforce that reparation if it be withheld. He may not have the power to enforce it, but the whole civilized world concurs in saying, that the power, if possessed, is rightfully used.[5]

In a state of nature, these individuals may contract, their contracts are obligatory, and force may rightfully be employed to coerce the party who has broken his engagement.

What is the effect of society upon these rights? When men unite together and form a government, do they surrender their right to contract, as well as their right to enforce the observance of contracts? . . . [I]ndividuals do not derive from government their right to contract, but bring that right with them into society; that obligation is not conferred on contracts by positive law, but is intrinsic, and is conferred by the act of the parties. This results from the right which every man retains to acquire property, to dispose of that property according to his own judgment, and to pledge himself for a future act. These rights are not given by society, but are brought into it. The right of coercion is necessarily surrendered to government, and this surrender imposes on government the correlative duty of furnishing a remedy.[6] The right to regulate contracts, to prescribe

---

[4] Editor's Note: Justice Marshall powerfully demonstrates that law and the coercive power thereof requires more than just might or naked power. In order for there to be justice, the coercive power of the law must be coupled with a right. In this case, the right is the right to enter into to contracts and have them enforced. Again, contra to the positivist position, Justice Marshall sees this right as deriving from the law of nature and nature's God as opposed to only from the civil government.

[5] Editor's Note: *See* the treaties referenced earlier between the rulers of the Philistines and Abraham and later Isaac as examples.

[6] Editor's Note: Marshall is here referring to the fact that the so-called "power of the sword" that the civil magistrate wields, which means that only the civil magistrate

rules by which they shall be evidenced, to prohibit such as may be deemed mischievous, is unquestionable, and has been universally exercised. So far as this power has restrained the original right of individuals to bind themselves by contract, it is restrained; but beyond these actual restraints the original power remains unimpaired.

This reasoning is, undoubtedly, much strengthened by the authority of those writers on natural and national law, whose opinions have been viewed with profound respect by, the wisest men of the present, and of past ages.

NOTES AND QUESTIONS

1. Ultimate Origins of Contract Law. Justice Marshall clearly believed that the right to and obligation of contract is derived not from the civil magistrate but rather from the law of nature and nature's God. He argues that this right and obligation is bound up in the nature of mankind. Do you agree? Do you think that the right to and obligation of contract is more than just a positive law of the state?

Assuming that Justice Marshall is right and that something about the very nature of mankind gives rise to the right to contract, where did that come from? To state it differently, why is the right to contract a part of the inherent rights of man? As discussed previously, I would submit that it is derived from mankind's stewardship-dominion duties and the image of God in man. God is a promise-making and keeping God. The Bible is full of and centered around God's promises to mankind and His keeping of those promises, most ultimately of course in the Lord Jesus Christ. Accordingly, as humans, we bear the image of God and, like our Creator, we can bind ourselves to contracts and, when we do, we are obligated to keep them. Accordingly, the ultimate source and origin of contract law is found in the nature of God Himself.

_____

_____

_____

_____

_____

_____

---

may use this coercive power on other people. I may not enforce a contract myself by imposing a fine on my neighbor who I believe to have breached his agreement with me. Rather, I must petition the civil magistrate for redress. The civil magistrate bears the sword as God's avenger; I do not. *See Romans* 12:19-13:5.

2. The Contracts Clause. The Founding Fathers clearly felt that the right to and enforcement of contracts was very important. Article I, Section 10, Clause 1 of the United States Constitution provides that "No State shall . . . pass any Law impairing the Obligation of Contracts." This clause was at issue in *Ogden v. Saunders* (in a portion of the opinion edited out.) Further, in the famous case of *Fletcher v. Peck*, 10 U.S. 87 (1810), Chief Justice John Marshall, writing for a six-to-one majority, declared a Georgia law unconstitutional because it violated the Contracts Clause. For an interesting discussion of the Contracts Clause and its decline in importance in recent years, *see* James W. Ely, Jr., *Whatever Happened to the Contracts Clause?*, 4 Charleston L. Rev. 371 (2010). As Prof. Ely points out, the Contracts Clause was once one of the most important provisions in the Constitution for limiting the power of the civil magistrate. Why do you think a clause that was so important to the Founders and so important in the early centuries of the Republic has fallen into such disfavor and disuse in the twentieth and twenty-first centuries?

_____

_____

_____

_____

_____

_____

3. Sacredness of Promises. Since God makes and keeps His promises, He (and derivately other people) expects us to keep our promises. We therefore can say that contracts are sacred because God expects us to fulfill what we promise. *See, e.g., Numbers* 30:2, *Deuteronomy* 23:21, and *Ecclesiastes* 5:1-7.

Since promises are sacred, contracts, as a subset of promises that are enforceable by the civil government, are also sacred. Therefore, a just civil government would seek to encourage contract-keeping and punish or discourage contract-breaking. Not surprisingly, a society that has a history of making and keeping promises and contracts is a blessed society. Its commerce will be more robust making all members better off, and its community will be stronger. This should be expected because we know that God's commands are not burdensome but are rather for our good. *See* 1 *John* 5:2-3.

Americans used to view promises as sacred. We used to be a faithful society, but in many ways we are/are becoming a faithless society. We used to be a society where one's promise or word was one's bond—it meant something. If someone agreed to do something, they felt very strongly that they should keep their promise. Handshake deals used to be common because a person's handshake meant that he had bound himself and would keep his promise.

Unfortunately, our society has departed from this level of integrity and we no longer see ourselves bound by our word. This shows up in a number of ways and examples are so numerous as to make examples unnecessary. In many ways, we have become a society of liars. It has undermined our trust in each other, and it is already and will continue to have enormous negative effects on our commerce and communities.

However, before rushing to judge others, it is helpful to consider our own hearts. Keeping your word is often difficult, and we may share our societal predilection for keeping our word only when it is easy and benefits us. In that regard, consider the following example.

In discussing the fact that we have become a faithless society that does not keep its word, Larry Burkett in *Business by the Book*, relates this example:

> I recall a time when my father, who was an electrician, agreed to rewire a neighbor's house for about $2,000. In the midst of the job he found that he had underbid by several hundred dollars and, at the same time, the cost of materials jumped because of a copper shortage. On a $2,000 job, my father stood to lose nearly $1,200, a sizable sum in the early fifties.

Larry Burkett, *Business By The Book: Complete Guide of Biblical Principles for the Workplace* 75 (2006). What would you do in a situation like this? Would you keep your word and fulfill the contract, or would you look to get out of the deal? What would the Bible say about how to handle this situation? (By the way, Larry Burkett's dad kept his word.)[7]

_____

_____

_____

_____

_____

4. Keeping Your Word. The Bible clearly indicates that Christians should be people of the truth. We should keep our word and fulfill our vows. *See, e.g., Exodus* 20:16, *Leviticus* 19:11, *Psalm* 15:1-4 and 58:3, *Proverbs* 6:16-19, *Ecclesiastes* 5:4-7, *Matthew* 5:33-37, *Ephesians*

---

[7] This is just one of many great examples that Larry Burkett gives in his book of how hard it can be to keep our word. They are certainly worth reading and reflecting upon.

4:25, and *Colossians* 3:9. However, often we all get busy in life and things sneak up on us. Therefore, it is good to plan in advance to do certain things and perhaps implement certain policies that will help us to keep our word and not overcommit or otherwise get in a situation where we are looking to "get out of" promises that we have made. We want to see these principles (i.e., the sacredness of the promise) reflected in our legal system, and we therefore need to live our lives in such a way that we, and organizations that we have control over, reflect these principles. For example, Larry Burkett suggests several guidelines for helping us to keep our word in *Business by the Book* such as "when in doubt, say no" and "don't book too far ahead." Can you think of others? How would you go about creating a culture of promise-keeping in any organization where you work or have authority?

_____

_____

_____

_____

_____

_____

CHAPTER 4
CAPACITY TO CONTRACT AND
THE COMMON LAW

The binding nature of contracts comes, in part, from the fact that they are voluntarily entered into by people bearing the image of God. This voluntariness is important. We are not required by God to make promises to others, but, when we voluntarily do so, we bind ourselves and should keep our word.

Generally speaking, the common law of contracts has viewed certain persons as being unable, for a number of reasons, to voluntarily enter into a contract and bind themselves. This is generally referred to as a lack of capacity to contract. Or, to state it as a rule, in order for one to bind himself to a contract he must have the requisite capacity to contract. The following case addresses this issue in the common scenario of a minor (generally in America this is now one under the age of 18) purchasing goods and later wanting to "get out of" of the contract.

Dodson by Dodson v. Shrader
824 S.W.2d 545 (Tenn. 1992)

This is an action to disaffirm the contract of a minor for the purchase of a pick-up truck and for a refund of the purchase price. The issue is whether the minor is entitled to a full refund of the money he paid or whether the seller is entitled to a setoff for the decrease in value of the pick-up truck while it was in the possession of the minor.

In early April of 1987, Joseph Eugene Dodson, then 16 years of age, purchased a used 1984 pick-up truck from Burns and Mary Shrader. The Shraders owned and operated Shrader's Auto Sales in Columbia, Tennessee. Dodson paid $4,900 in cash for the truck, using money he borrowed from his girlfriend's grandmother. At the time of the purchase there was no inquiry by the Shraders, and no misrepresentation by Mr.

Dodson, concerning his minority. However, Mr. Shrader did testify that at the time he believed Mr. Dodson to be 18 or 19 years of age.

In December 1987, nine (9) months after the date of purchase, the truck began to develop mechanical problems. A mechanic diagnosed the problem as a burnt valve, but could not be certain without inspecting the valves inside the engine. Mr. Dodson did not want, or did not have the money, to effect these repairs. He continued to drive the truck despite the mechanical problems. One month later, in January, the truck's engine "blew up" and the truck became inoperable.

Mr. Dodson parked the vehicle in the front yard at his parents home where he lived. He contacted the Shraders to rescind the purchase of the truck and requested a full refund. The Shraders refused to accept the tender of the truck or to give Mr. Dodson the refund requested.

Mr. Dodson then filed an action in general sessions court seeking to rescind the contract and recover the amount paid for the truck. . . . Mr. Shrader, through counsel, declined to accept the tender of the truck without compensation for its depreciation. Before the circuit court could hear the case, the truck, while parked in Dodson's front yard, was struck on the left front fender by a hit-and-run driver. At the time of the circuit court trial, according to Shrader, the truck was worth only $500 due to the damage to the engine and the left front fender.

The case was heard in the circuit court in November 1988. The trial judge, based on previous common-law decisions and, under the doctrine of *stare decisis* reluctantly granted the rescission. The Shraders were ordered, upon tender and delivery of the truck, to reimburse the $4,900 purchase price to Mr. Dodson. The Shraders appealed.

The Court of Appeals . . . affirmed; . . .

The earliest recorded case in this State, on the issue involved, appears to be in *Wheaton v. East,* 13 Tenn. 35 (5 Yeager 41) (1833). In pronouncing the rule to apply governing infant's contracts, the court said:

> We do not perceive that any general rule, as to contracts which are void and voidable, can be stated with more precision that is done by Lord Ch. J. Eyre in *Keane v. Boycott,* 2 H. Black, 511, and quoted with approbation by Judge Story, 1 Mason's Rep. 82, and by Chancellor Kent, 2 Com. 193, which is this: "that when the court can pronounce the contract to be to the infant's prejudice, it is void, and when to his benefit, as for necessaries, it is good; and when the contract is of any uncertain nature, as to benefit or prejudice, it is voidable only, at the election of the infant." . . .

The law on the subject of the protection of infant's rights has been slow to evolve. However, in *Human v. Hartsell,* 24 Tenn.App. 678, 148 S.W.2d 634, 636 (1940) the Court of Appeals noted:

> The last case in Tennessee holding a minor's contract void and adopting as the criterion for determining whether a given contract is void or only voidable [based upon] the prejudicial, uncertain or beneficial effect upon the rights and interests of the minor, appears to be the case of *Robinson v. Coulter,* supra, [90 Tenn. 705, 18 S.W. 250] decided November 12, 1891. In *Tuck v. Payne,* 159 Tenn. 192, 17 S.W.2d 8, in an opinion by Mr. Justice McKinney, the modern rule that contracts of infants are not void but only voidable and subject to be disaffirmed by the minor either before or after attaining majority appears to have been favored.
>
> Under this rule the efforts of early authorities to classify contracts as beneficial or harmful and determine whether they are void or only voidable upon the basis of such classification are abandoned in favor of permitting the infant himself when he has become of age to determine what contracts are and what are not to his interest and liking. He is thus permitted to assume the burden of a contract, clearly disadvantageous to him, if he deems himself under a moral obligation to do so.
>
> The adoption of this rule does not lead to any retrenchment of the infant's rights but gives him the option of invoking contracts found to be advantageous but which, if held void, could not be enforced against the other party to the contract. Thus the minor can secure the advantage of contracts advantageous to himself and be relieved of the effect of an injudicious contract.

In *Tuck,* supra, 17 S.W.2d at p. 9, the court applied the rule based upon the maxims that he who seeks equity must do equity, that he who comes into equity must come with clean hands, that no one can take advantage of his own wrong, that he that has committed inequity shall not have equity, and that minors will not be permitted to use the shield of infancy as a cover, or turn it into a sword with which to injure others dealing with them in good faith.

As noted by the Court of Appeals, the rule in Tennessee, as modified, is in accord with the majority rule on the issue among our sister states. This rule is based upon the underlying purpose of the "infancy doctrine" which is to protect minors from their lack of judgment and "from squandering their wealth through improvident contracts with crafty adults who would take advantage of them in the marketplace." *Halbman v. Lemke,* 99 Wis.2d 241, 245, 298 N.W.2d 562, 564 (1980).

There is, however, a modern trend among the states, either by judicial action or by statute, in the approach to the problem of balancing the rights of minors against those of innocent merchants. As a result, two minority rules have developed which allow the other party to a contract with a minor to refund less than the full consideration paid in the event of rescission.

The first of these minority rules is called the "Benefit Rule." . . . The rule holds that, upon rescission, recovery of the full purchase price is subject to a deduction for the minor's use of the merchandise. This rule recognizes that the traditional rule in regard to necessaries has been extended so far as to hold an infant bound by his contracts, where he failed to restore what he has received under them to the extent of the benefit actually derived by him from what he has received from the other party to the transaction. . . .

The other minority rule holds that the minor's recovery of the full purchase price is subject to a deduction for the minor's "use" of the consideration he or she received under the contract, or for the "depreciation" or "deterioration" of the consideration in his or her possession. . . .

We are impressed by the statement made by the Arizona Appeals Court in *Valencia v. White,* [654 P.2d 287 (Ariz. App. 1982)], citing the Court of Appeals of Ohio in *Haydocy Pontiac Inc. v. Lee,* 19 Ohio App.2d 217, 250 N.E.2d 898 (1969):

> At a time when we see young persons between 18 and 21 years of age demanding and assuming more responsibilities in their daily lives; when we see such persons emancipated, married, and raising families; when we see such persons charged with the responsibility for committing crimes; when we see such persons being sued in tort claims for acts of negligence; when we see such persons subject to military service; when we see such persons engaged in business and acting in almost all other respects as an adult, it seems timely to re-examine the case law pertaining to contractual rights and responsibilities of infants to see if the law as pronounced and applied by the courts should be redefined.

. . .

Upon serious reflection we are convinced that a modified form of the Oregon rule should be adopted in this State concerning the rights and responsibilities of minors in their business dealings. [The Oregon rule is the second or "other" minority rule listed above by the court that holds that the minor's recovery is subject to a deduction for the minor's use or the depreciation of the article.]

This is no quantum leap in the evolution of the common law. As early as 1842, in the case of *Jacob v. The State,* 22 Tenn. 372, 388, 3 Humphreys 514 (1842), Justice Turley delivered a profound dissertation on the policy and principles of the common law:

> The common law has been aptly called the *"lex non scripta,"* because it is a rule prescribed by the common consent and agreement of the community as one applicable to its different relations, and capable of preserving the peace, good order, and harmony of society, and rendering unto every one that which of right belongs to him. Its sources are to be found in the usages, habits, manners, and customs of a people. Its seat is in the breast of the judges who are its expositors and expounders. Every nation must of necessity have its common law, let it be called by what name it may, and it will be simple or complicated in its details, as society is simple or complicated in its relations. A few plain and practical rules will do for a wandering horde of savages, but they must and will be much more extensively ramified when civilization has polished, and commerce and arts and agriculture enriched, a nation. The common law of a country will, therefore, never be entirely stationary, but will be modified, and extended by analogy, construction and custom, so as to embrace new relations, springing up from time to time, from an amelioration or change of society. The present common law of England is as dissimilar from that of Edward III as is the present state of society. And we apprehend that no one could be found to contend that hundreds of principles, which have in more modern times been examined, argued, and determined by the judges, are not principles of the common law, because not found in the books of that period. They are held to be great and immutable principles, which have slumbered in their repositories, because the occasion called for their exposition had not arisen. The common law, then, is not like the statute law, fixed, and immutable but by positive enactment, except where a principle has been adjudged as the rule of action.
>
> If, then, one generation be not so hedged in by the principles of the common law, established by another, as to be prohibited from extending them, by analogy and construction, to new relations and modifications of society, by

what principle shall a sovereign state, which has adopted the common law of another as one of its rule of action, be so prohibited?

Such, then, is the common law, that though principles once established by judicial determination can only be changed by legislative enactment, yet such is its malleability (if we may use the expression) that new principles may be developed, and old ones extended, by analogy, so as to embrace newly-created relations and changes produced by time and circumstances. . . .

The late Justice Joseph W. Henry, past member and former Chief Justice of this Court stated the message of the flexibility of the common law in more modern language in *Dunn v. Palermo,* 522 S.W.2d 679, 688 (Tenn.1975), as follows:

This Court in the past has not hesitated to depart from the rigid common law where "the reason for the common law rule does not exist." *Brown v. Shelby,* 206 Tenn. 71, 332 S.W.2d 166 (1960).

The common law does not have the force of Holy Writ; it is not a last will and testament, nor is it a cadaver embalmed in perpetuity, nor is it to be treated like the sin of Judah—"written with a pen of iron and with the point of a diamond." *Jeremiah* 17:1.

Former Chief Justice Frantz of Colorado, in his dissenting opinion in *Tesone v. School Dist. No. Re–2, In County of Boulder,* 152 Colo. 596, 384 P.2d 82 (1963), made this erudite observation on the common law:
"The common law of America is evolutionary; it is not static and immutable. It is in constant growth, going through mutations in adapting itself to changing conditions and in improving and refining doctrine. By its very nature, it seeks perfection in the achievement of justice."
This is an eloquent description of the greatness and the glory of the common law.

We state the rule to be followed hereafter, in reference to a contract of a minor, to be where the minor has not been overreached in any way, and there has been no undue influence, and the contract is a fair and reasonable one, and the minor has actually paid money on the purchase price, and taken and used the article purchased, that he ought not to be permitted to recover the amount actually paid, without allowing the vender of the goods reasonable compensation for the use of, depreciation, and willful or negligent damage to the article purchased, while in his hands. If there has been any fraud or imposition on the part of the seller or if the contract is unfair, or any unfair advantage has been taken of the minor inducing him to make the purchase, then the rule does not apply. Whether there has been such an overreaching on the part of the seller, and the fair market value of the property returned, would always, in any case, be a question for the trier of fact. This rule will fully and fairly protect the minor against injustice or imposition, and at the same time it will be fair to a business person who has dealt with such minor in good faith.

This rule is best adapted to modern conditions under which minors are permitted to, and do in fact, transact a great deal of business for themselves, long before they have reached the age of legal majority. Many young people work and earn money and collect it and spend it oftentimes without any oversight or restriction. The law does not question their right to buy if they have the money to pay for their purchases. It seems intolerably burdensome for everyone concerned if merchants and business people cannot deal with them safely, in a fair and reasonable way. Further, it does not appear consistent with practice of proper moral influence upon young people, tend to encourage honesty and integrity, or lead them to a good and useful business future, if they are taught that they can make purchases with their own money, for their own benefit, and after paying for them, and using them until they are worn out and destroyed, go back and compel the vendor to return to them what they have paid upon the purchase price. Such a doctrine can only lead to the corruption of principles and encourage young people in habits of trickery and dishonesty.

. . .

We note that in this case, some nine (9) months after the date of purchase, the truck purchased by the plaintiff began to develop mechanical problems. Plaintiff was informed of the probable nature of the difficulty which apparently involved internal problems in the engine. He continued to drive the vehicle until the engine "blew up" and the truck became inoperable. Whether or not this involved gross negligence or intentional conduct on his part is a matter for determination at the trial level. It is not possible to determine from this record whether a counterclaim for tortious damage to the vehicle was asserted. After the first tender of the vehicle was made by plaintiff, and refused by the defendant, the truck was damaged by a hit-and-run driver while parked on plaintiff's property. The amount of that damage and the liability for that amount between the purchaser and the vendor, as well as the fair market value of the vehicle at the time of tender, is also an issue for the trier of fact.

The case is remanded to the trial court for further proceedings in accordance with this judgment. The costs on appellate review are assessed equally between the parties.

NOTES AND QUESTIONS

1. What would you do? In the position of the Tennessee Supreme Court, what would you have done? Should the rule be that Dodson be able to return the truck and get all of his money back? Is this just? If not, what should the rule be? What is the purpose of the requirement of capacity anyway, and how should it be applied in this case?

_____

_____

_____

_____

_____

_____

2. Changing the Common Law. The court in this opinion changes the common law of Tennessee by adopting a modified version of the Oregon rule. In so doing, the course spends a good deal of time discussing the nature of the common law and how it can and should change at times. Since we have been studying the common law of contracts, it is a good idea to consider what we mean by the phrase "common law" and whether and to what extent it can and should change.

First, it is often said that the common law is "judge-made law" as opposed to statutory law, i.e., laws enacted by the legislature. While this statement is so often used as to become a cliché, it does not match the historical view of the common law in the Western legal tradition. In the Western legal tradition, judge's are thought to discover, not make, the common law. In his excellent book *God, Man, and Law: The Biblical Principles*, Dean Herbert Titus describes the historic view of the common law:

> Rather [than following Jefferson's more positivist view of the common law], America's legal scholars affirmed time and time again that the Common Law "was derived from the law of nature and of revelation, those rules and maxims of immutable truth and justice, which arise from the eternal

fitness of things, which need only be understood, to be submitted to, as they are themselves the highest authority."

. . .

The "law of nature and of revelation" was understood to be objective norms imposed by Almighty God on all mankind. Even Jefferson appealed to such an objective legal order when he wrote the Declaration of Independence [and used the phrase "the laws of nature and nature's God."]

The Declaration's appeal rested not upon any novel claim, but upon the very foundation of the common law, articulated most consistently and persuasively by Sir William Blackstone in his *Commentaries on the Law of England*.

At the time of the American Revolution and for over one hundred years afterward, Blackstone's *Commentaries* served as the basic text for lawyers and law students in America.

. . .

In his introductory discourse on law, Blackstone remarked that "the revealed or divine law . . . to be found only in the Holy Scriptures . . . [is] really a part of the original law of nature" [and] this "law of nature . . . is binding over all the globe, in all countries and at all times."

. . .

Because Blackstone claimed that the common law embodied the law of nature as revealed by God's created order and by God's Word, he claimed that judges did not make the common law, they only discovered, stated, and applied it. A judge's opinion or order in a particular case, therefore, was not, according to Blackstone, law: it was only evidence of law.

. . .

While Blackstone believed that a judge's opinion was not law, he believed that those opinions deserved great respect and bound others in like cases unless they were contrary to the law. This view is known as the common law doctrine of *stare decisis*.[1]

Accordingly, we see that the common law is not "judge-made" law. Rather, the common law is those rules, maxims, and principles of immutable truth and justice, which are derived from the laws of nature and nature's god and are therefore binding on all people, in all countries, and at all times. The common law is not made by judges, but rather it is discovered, stated, and applied to specific situations. Judges' opinions are not law, but they are entitled to much respect as evidence of the law and reasoned applications of the law to a particular set of facts.

This leads naturally to the second issue raised by the case: whether and to what extent can the common law change? A short answer is that the common law itself cannot change—it is eternal and immutable. The eternal and universal principles that comprise the common law are just that—eternal and universal. However, the application of those principles can certainly change. Further, prior opinions could have wrongly understood the common law, wrongly stated it, or wrongly applied it. Obviously, in that case, there may be a change, but the change is in the development of the opinions—not the common law itself. Finally, as societies progress, we grow in our understanding of the law by building on those who came before us. Accordingly, some development in common-law jurisprudence should therefore be expected. For more on the nature of the common law, its progression, and the law of nature and nature's God, *see* Jeffrey Tuomala, Marbury v. Madison *and the Foundation of Law*, 4 Liberty U. L. Rev. 297 (2010), Albert W. Alschuler, *From Blackstone to Holmes: The Revolt Against Natural Law*, 36 Pepp. L. Rev. 491 (2009), Herbert W. Titus, *God, Man, and Law: The Biblical Principles* 1-63 (1994).

All of that said, did the court get it right here? Should the common law be changed in this way? If so, what are the universal principles and what part of the decision is an application of those principles? Finally, does the Bible ever speak to contractual capacity or the like? *See, e.g., Numbers* 1:3 (males must be 20 or older to go to war) and 30:1-16 (on the binding nature of men's vows, married women's vows, and the vows of daughter's living in their father's home).

_____

_____

_____

_____

_____

_____

---

[1] Herbert W. Titus, *God, Man, and Law: The Biblical Principles* 41-60 (1994) (citations and much other material omitted).

CHAPTER 5
WRITTEN CONTRACTS, LEGAL PROFESSIONALS, AND STEWARDING DREAMS

Lyrick Studios, Inc. v. Big Idea Productions, Inc.
420 F.3d 388 (2005)

Appellee Lyrick Studios, Inc. ("Lyrick") contends that appellant Big Idea Productions, Inc. ("Big Idea") breached their agreement under which Big Idea provided Lyrick with an exclusive license to distribute children's cartoon programs. Lyrick sued over this breach, and the jury found in its favor. Big Idea appeals, arguing that Lyrick cannot satisfy the requirement that all transfers of copyright (such as exclusive licenses) must be in writing and signed by the transferor. Because there is no sufficient writing here, we reverse the judgment.

Phil Vischer founded Appellant Big Idea Productions, Inc. to finance and market "VeggieTales," a computer-animated Christian-themed children's cartoon he created, featuring the characters Bob the Tomato and Larry the Cucumber. Originally, Big Idea independently distributed VeggieTales to members of an organization called the Christian Bookstores Association ("CBA"). The programs were successful, and Big Idea eventually entered into a contract with a third party to distribute to the CBA. VeggieTales' sales continued to grow.

With this success, Big Idea wanted to sell its products to a larger audience. To do this, Big Idea began negotiating with Lyrick Studios, which had experience with its own successful children's programs. In February 1997, Tim Clott, Lyrick's CEO, sent Big Idea the first of three documents that are critical to this case. This document was a proposal for distribution of VeggieTales to the "general marketplace." It ended with the caveat that "for both of our protection, no contract will exist until both parties have executed a formal agreement." Big Idea's vice president of licensing and development, Bill Haljun, sent the second critical document-a fax that listed several issues still to be decided. The next day, the parties discussed the issues in a phone call and agreed to resolve them. Haljun faxed Clott a few days later, noting that "Phil is ecstatic."

Shortly afterwards, Lyrick prepared a 16-page contract. This draft agreement was never signed. In fact, several draft contracts (and suggested revisions to the drafts) were sent back and forth over the years. There were several sticking points, including DVD distribution rights, rights to stuffed animals, the possibility of a "key man" provision, and even the term of the contract. The parties agree that no formal "long-form" contract was ever signed.

Despite lacking a formal signed contract, in March 1998, Lyrick began distributing VeggieTales videocassettes. The cassettes were immediately successful; both parties made a significant profit from the relationship.

The negotiations over a written contract continued until June 1999, when the fourth and final draft was prepared by Lyrick. Like the other drafts, this one was never signed. At some point around this time, the parties' relationship became strained. One point of contention involved the rights to stuffed animals, or as the parties referred to them, plush. The parties eventually signed an agreement ("the plush letter") transferring plush rights in VeggieTales from Lyrick to Big Idea.

In March 2001, Lyrick was acquired by HIT Entertainment, a London-based children's entertainment company, but it continued to distribute VeggieTales. In December 2001, Big Idea informed Lyrick that it was going to use a new distributor. In response, Lyrick sued Big Idea.

This lawsuit is primarily based on Lyrick's claims that Big Idea breached its exclusive license/distribution agreement by entering into an agreement with the new distributor. During discovery, Big Idea produced a document that Lyrick now contends is the third crucial document—a November 1997 internal memorandum by Bill Haljun. Haljun wrote this memo in response to a Big Idea employee's question about the 10-year term with Lyrick. In his memo, Haljun replied that "[w]e agreed over the phone to his contract .... I would say that we have an agreement in force." Lyrick had not seen this internal memorandum before litigation.

The case proceeded to trial. After the close of Lyrick's evidence, Big Idea moved for judgment as a matter of law, arguing that any contract for an exclusive license of a copyrighted work, such as VeggieTales, had to be in writing. The district court denied this motion, and the case went to the jury. The jury found that there had been a contract and that Big Idea had breached it. As a result, the jury awarded Lyrick damages of $9,071,973 for lost profits on videocassettes and DVDs. The district court entered judgment for this amount, along with $750,000 in attorney's fees. The judgment amount also included $14,540 in damages for breach of the plush letter; Big Idea agreed to this $14,540 award before trial and does not appeal it. The court also permitted Lyrick to collect on a $500,000 bond Big Idea posted when it obtained a preliminary injunction preventing Lyrick from distributing VeggieTales products. Big Idea now appeals the district court's denial of its motion for judgment as a matter of law. We review this ruling de novo. Judgment as a matter of law is proper when "there is no legally sufficient basis for a reasonable jury to find for [a] party on [an] issue."

Under § 204(a) of the Copyright Act, "[a] transfer of copyright ownership, other than by operation of law, is not valid unless an instrument of conveyance, or a note or memorandum of the transfer, is in writing and signed by the owner of the rights conveyed or such owner's duly authorized agent." 17 U.S.C. § 204(a). A grant of an exclusive license is considered a "transfer of copyright ownership." 17 U.S.C. § 101 (2005). Section 204(a)'s requirement, while sometimes called the copyright statute of frauds, is in fact different from a statute of frauds. Rather than serving an evidentiary function and making otherwise valid agreements unenforceable, under § 204(a) "a transfer of copyright is simply 'not valid' without a writing." *Id.* The writing in question "doesn't have to be the Magna Charta; a one-line pro forma statement will do." *Effects Assocs., Inc. v. Cohen,* 908 F.2d 555, 557 (9th Cir.1990). Nor does the writing have to contain any particular language. *Radio Television Espanola S.A. v. New World Entm't, Ltd.,* 183 F.3d 922, 927 (9th Cir.1999) ("No magic words must be included in a document to satisfy § 204(a)."). It must, however, show an agreement to transfer copyright. *Id.; see also Playboy Enters., Inc. v. Dumas,* 53 F.3d 549, 564 (2d Cir.1995). An after-the-fact writing can validate an agreement from the date of its inception, at least against challenges to the agreement by third parties. *Billy-Bob Teeth, Inc. v. Novelty, Inc.,* 329 F.3d 586, 591 (7th Cir.2003); *Magnuson v. Video Yesteryear,* 85 F.3d 1424, 1429 (9th Cir.1996); *Imperial Residential Design, Inc. v. Palms Dev. Group, Inc.,* 70 F.3d 96, 99 (11th Cir.1995); *Eden Toys, Inc. v. Florelee Undergarment Co., Inc.,* 697 F.2d 27, 36 (2d Cir.1982). The parties both agree that the issue whether the parties' undisputed writings satisfy § 204(a) is one of law. *Cf. Television Espanola,* 183 F.3d at 924 (deciding the issue on a motion for summary judgment); *Konigsberg,* 16 F.3d at 356 (deciding the issue on a motion to dismiss).

The writing requirement serves several purposes. First, it ensures that a copyright will not be inadvertently transferred. *Effects Assocs.,* 908 F.2d at 557. Second, it "forces a party who wants to use the copyrighted work to negotiate with the creator to determine precisely what rights are being transferred and at what price." *Id.* Third, it provides a guide for resolving disputes; the parties can look to the writing to determine whether a use is improper. *Id.* In this way, the writing requirement "enhances predictability and certainty of copyright ownership- 'Congress'[s] paramount goal' when it revised the [Copyright] Act in 1976." *Id.* (quoting *Community for Creative Non-Violence v. Reid,* 490 U.S. 730, 749, 109 S.Ct. 2166, 104 L.Ed.2d 811 (1989)).

Here the parties dispute whether Big Idea and Lyrick have a writing that meets § 204(a)'s requirement. Lyrick contends that § 204(a) is satisfied with a series of documents—the letters between Haljun and Clott and the internal Haljun memorandum. Big Idea responds that the letters were just proposals and never showed a final agreement. Big Idea also argues that Haljun's internal memo is not the kind of writing that can satisfy § 204(a).

Resolving this issue requires us to examine the documents. In the first document-the February 1997 letter from Tim Clott of Lyrick to Bill Haljun of Big Idea—the opening paragraph describes the letters contents as "our proposal." The rest of the letter sets out provisions such as territory, term, rights, products, and the distribution of proceeds. The final paragraph contains some critical language: "If the above terms are acceptable to you we will begin drafting a formal agreement. (Of course, for both of our protection, no contract will exist until both parties have executed a formal agreement.)"

The second document that Lyrick relies on is Bill Haljun's faxed response. The cover sheet for this fax states, "Here is our agreement to proceed and the remaining issues and understandings which we need to resolve prior to signing a formal document." The faxed letter reads, in part, "We agree to proceed to formalize this relationship as quickly as possible with binding agreements, subject to the following clarifications and additions. Hopefully, we can resolve these issues promptly and begin the selling process . . . with the July trade show." A list of changes and proposals followed.

The final document is an internal memorandum written by Haljun in November 1997, over six months after his fax and directly responding to a concern about the proposed 10-year term. It describes the parties' negotiations and indicates that, "We agreed over the phone to his contract and thanked him very much." In recalling the discussions, Haljun indicates that Big Idea requested a minimum volume term, but Lyrick did not accept it. Continuing, the memo states that Big Idea suggested some revisions to the draft long-form contract and that Lyrick had not yet responded to those revisions. The memo concludes with language that Lyrick finds critical:

Net of all this—when we told Tim Clott we accepted his proposal and we would go forward on that basis, and they have printed catalogs, represented our products and gotten them on television, designed plush, and paid for some research, I would say that we have an agreement in force.

This memo was never sent to Lyrick. In fact, Lyrick saw it for the first time during discovery.

Lyrick contends that these three documents constitute a sufficient written agreement. This assertion raises two primary issues. First, do the first two faxes indicate that they are preliminary in nature or do they contain an actual contract? Second, can Haljun's internal memorandum constitute a "a note or memorandum of the transfer?"

The two 1997 faxes, standing alone, do not show that the parties entered into a final agreement to provide Lyrick with an exclusive license to distribute VeggieTales programs. The February fax from Lyrick indicates that it is a proposal. More importantly, it expressly states, "Of course, for both of our protection, no contract will exist until both parties have executed a formal agreement." Big Idea's fax in response also indicates a lack of finality, providing that, "We agree to proceed to formalize this relationship as quickly as possible with binding agreements." This statement indicates that the fax itself is not a binding agreement. Section 204(a) requires some language of finality. *Radio Television Espanola,* 183 F.3d at 928. Finally, the continuing debate over the draft long-form contracts concerned some of the terms in the 1997 faxes (such as the term and the actual products to be distributed), which further shows that the faxes were not final contracts.

Lyrick attempts to cure these problems by turning to the internal Haljun memo. Lyrick argues that "[i]f a writing *executed* after litigation has commenced is sufficient to satisfy Section 204(a), a writing executed shortly after the agreement was reached but *communicated to* the transferee after litigation has commenced should also be sufficient . . . ." Lyrick thus tries to fit this case in the line of cases where a post-transfer writing has met § 204(a)'s requirements. We initially note that when courts have found the post-deal writing sufficient, the party challenging the writing has been an alleged infringer who is an outsider to the deal. *Billy-Bob Teeth,* 329 F.3d at 590 (rival novelty tooth manufacturer); *Magnuson,* 85 F.3d at 1427 (unauthorized distributor); *Eden Toys,* 697 F.2d at 30-31 (manufacturer of a nightshirt with a similar print to licensed one); *Kaplan Co., Inc. v. Panaria Int'l, Inc.,* No. 96-Civ.-7973, 1998 WL 603225, at *2 (S.D.N.Y. Sept. 11, 1998) (infringing third-party manufacturer). In that situation, courts are hesitant to allow an outside infringer to challenge the timing or technicalities of the copyright transfer. *See Billy-Bob Teeth,* 329 F.3d at 592-93; *Magnuson,* 85 F.3d at 1428-29; *Eden Toys,* 697 F.2d at 36. That situation is different from the situation here, where the parties to the alleged contract disagree about whether a valid agreement actually exists. Thus, the analysis in these cases does not apply here, and the cases themselves are not relevant.

On the other hand, two Ninth Circuit cases are relevant, each for different reasons. One, *Konigsberg International, Inc. v. Rice*, addresses a post-transfer letter in the context of a dispute between the parties to the alleged contract. 16 F.3d 355 (9th Cir.1994). The other, *Radio Television Espanola S.A. v. New World Entertainment, Ltd.*, concerns a purely internal memorandum that was not provided to the other party to the alleged transfer until litigation. 183 F.3d 922 (9th Cir.1999).

In *Konigsberg*, two movie producers entered into an oral agreement with the author Anne Rice. 16 F.3d at 356. Under this agreement, Rice would create a story, called a "bible," that "could form the basis for derivative works in various entertainment media." *Id*. Rice would then write a novel based on the bible and the producers would have two years of movie and television rights, with an option to extend. *Id*. A written contract was never signed, although Rice delivered the bible and in exchange received $50,000 from the producers. *Id*. Rice then wrote a successful novel, *The Mummy*, based on the bible, but the producers were not able to exercise their rights. *Id*. The producers claimed that Rice refused their attempts to exercise their option to extend. Therefore they sued. *Id*. The district court dismissed the case because there was no writing that satisfied § 204(a). *Id*. Rice then sent the producers' lawyer a letter stating, "[A]s far as I am concerned, these contracts, though never signed, were honored to the letter." *Id*. The producers tried to use this letter to reopen the case, arguing that this letter met § 204(a)'s writing requirements. *Id*.

The Ninth Circuit disagreed. It determined that Rice's letter was not a sufficient writing:

> Rice's letter was written three and a half years after the alleged oral agreement, a year and a half after its alleged term would have expired and 6 months into a contentious lawsuit. Thus, it was not substantially contemporaneous with the oral agreement. Nor was it a product of the parties' negotiations; it came far too late to provide any reference point for the parties' license disputes. In short, Rice's letter—though ill-advised—was not the type of writing contemplated by section 204 as sufficient to effect a transfer of the copyright to THE MUMMY.

Id. at 357. Here, the document is more contemporaneous, entered into during the course of the parties' exchange of the long-form contracts. But *Konigsberg* shows, however, that not all documents referring to the existence of a contract, or even admitting that an agreement existed, will constitute a sufficient note or memorandum of transfer.

Radio Television Espanola is much closer to the situation here. There a television company, Television Espanola, negotiated an exclusive license with a distributor for certain programs. *Radio Television Espanola,* 183 F.3d at 925. Afterwards, the distributor's negotiating agent drafted and signed an internal memo that listed the terms of the agreement. *Id.* This memo noted that the television company was to prepare the contracts. *Id.* Following this memo, the parties exchanged many letters, faxes, and memos, but never signed a contract. *Id.* Trying to overcome the lack of a formal signed contract, Television Espanola pointed to several different documents it claimed satisfied § 204(a). The first was a fax in which one of the distributor's executives referred to a deal between the parties. *Id.* at 927. The court concluded that this fax did not satisfy the writing requirement:

> Surely, the fax references a deal, but it does not specify anything about that deal or whether that deal is for an exclusive license for the program or for other broadcast rights. A mere reference to a deal without any information about the deal itself fails to satisfy the simple requirements of § 204(a). Without more, the comment in the Garcia fax is merely a part of negotiations rather than an "instrument of conveyance" or "memorandum of the transfer."

Id. (citation omitted). The second document that Television Espanola relied on was also a fax. *Id.* This fax, also from the distributor, discussed delivering episodes and concludes "[w]ith nothing further at this time, awaiting the contracts." *Id.* The court concluded that this fax, too, failed to satisfy § 204(a). *Id.* The court noted that the fax did not discuss the exclusive license and that "The statement that New World is waiting for the contracts 'undercuts the hint of finality' that the fax may otherwise contain." *Id.* at 928 (citing *Valente-Kritzer Video v. Pinckney,* 881 F.2d 772, 775 (9th Cir.1989)). Finally, Television Espanola claimed that two other documents were sufficient writings. The first document was the distributor's internal deal memo, describing the deal in some detail, including the term and the total fee. *Id.* The second document was a fax from Television Espanola asking the distributor to confirm the contract. *Id.* Yet the court found that these documents, even when taken together with the previous ones, did not contain "language indicating finality." *Id.* Rather, they discussed a pending contract and negotiations. *Id.*

In rejecting Television Espanola's claim, the Ninth Circuit noted an additional reason why the internal deal memorandum was not a sufficient writing. The memo could not have satisfied § 204(a) "because it was never communicated to Television Espanola." *Id.* at 928 n. 6. Again, not all writings will satisfy § 204(a)'s requirements.

In general, this case is similar to *Radio Television Espanola*-preliminary faxes indicated that a contract would be entered into but did not provide a final contract; an internal memo, never intended to be given to the other party, described some of the terms. To be sure, there are also several differences. Haljun's internal memo indicates that he agreed over the phone and that he would say that they had an agreement in force. This is somewhat more final than the internal memorandum in *Radio Television Espanola*. These differences, however, do not change the reasoning or the result.

In the end, we conclude that the faxes themselves do not set out a final signed contract. By their own language, they are part of negotiations: Lyrick's initial fax states that "no contract will exist until both parties have executed a formal agreement." Nor do the faxes satisfy the requirements when combined with Haljun's internal memo. Like the letter in *Konigsberg* and the memo in *Radio Television Espanola*, Haljun's memo is not the kind of memorandum of transfer envisioned by § 204(a). Satisfying § 204(a)'s writing requirement with a purely internal memo that was never intended to be provided to Lyrick would not further the copyright goals of predictability of ownership. *See Effects Assocs.*, 908 F.2d at 557.

Lyrick alternatively argues that the parties acted as if they had a deal for several years, making it unfair for Big Idea to rely on a "hyper-technical" § 204(a) argument. The Ninth Circuit rejected a similar argument in *Konigsberg* when it required a writing even in the face of ample evidence of an agreement, including that Rice had written the bible and had been paid for it. *Konigsberg*, 16 F.3d at 356. Section 204(a) requires a writing. Although Lyrick argues that enforcing this requirement would be unjust, we will not add an exception to the statute.

Attorney's Fees

Lyrick was awarded $750,000 in attorney's fees under Tex. Civ. Prac. & Rem.Code § 38.001, which permits a party to recover its attorney's fees for successful breach of contract claims. Big Idea asks us to reverse this amount and allow Lyrick to recover a reasonable amount to cover the fees for only the breach of the plush letter claim, not the breach of exclusive contract claim.

Lyrick contends that Big Idea stipulated that $750,000 was a reasonable amount of attorney's fees and thus the award should stand in full. We read the stipulation differently. In the parties' pretrial order, Big Idea agreed "that $750,000 is a reasonable and necessary amount for Lyrick to have incurred in the prosecution of its breach of contract *claims* in this action in the district court." (Emphasis added). This stipulation refers to both claims in the aggregate; it says nothing about the reasonable amount of fees for the breach of the plush letter by itself. We will remand the attorney's fees claim to the district court for a determination of a reasonable amount of fees for Lyrick's $14,540 recovery for breach of the plush letter.

Bond

[In this section of the opinion, the court vacated the lower court's order allowing Lyrick to execute on a bond that Big Idea has posted in relation to its motion for a preliminary injunction.]

Conclusion

For these reasons, we reverse the judgment of the district court, vacate the order permitting Lyrick to execute on the bond, and remand for consideration of attorney's fees and entry of an order for restitution of the bond.

REVERSED AND REMANDED.

NOTES AND QUESTIONS

1. Should All Contracts have to be in Writing to be Enforceable? As you know by now, not all contracts have to be in writing to be enforceable. Oral contracts and implied contracts are enforceable in many instances. Often, a writing is desirable not to make the contract enforceable but to deal with proof issues by making clear what the parties have agreed. That said, why should some contracts be required to be in writing and others not? Is this just? Should the law just require that all contracts be in writing to be enforceable? Why or why not?

_____

_____

_____

_____

_____

_____

2. A Statute of Frauds or No? The court in the above case asserts that while § 204(a) of the Copyright Act is "sometimes called the copyright statute of frauds, [it] is in fact different from a statute of frauds." What does the court mean by this? What is the difference between § 204(a) and a typical statute of frauds and why does it matter?

_____

_____

_____

_____

_____

_____

3. The Story Behind the Case and the Call to Help People Steward Their Dreams. The story of Phil Vischer, Big Idea Productions, Inc., and VeggieTales is compelling, and it just happens to be the back-story behind this case. Phil Vischer, the creator of VeggieTales and the founder of Big Idea Productions, Inc., wrote an excellent book Describing his experiences and the VeggieTales saga entitled *Me, Myself, & Bob: A True Story about God, Dreams, and Talking Vegetables* (2006).[8] This case and this story is worth considering for what it teaches us about being legal professionals and helping to shepherd people's gifts, abilities, time, treasure, and, yes, even dreams.

Here is how Mr. Vischer describes his dream in the introduction to his book:

> I had a dream. I wanted my stories to make the world a better place. I wanted to build the next Disney. Be the next Disney. And as of September 26, 2002, everything appeared to be working perfectly. I had led the team that created and launched VeggieTales, the most successful direct-to-video series in history. I had built the largest animation studio between the coasts. And that night found me standing in front of a cheering throng at the premier of our first animated feature film, choking back tears as I stared out at the happy faces of hundreds of friends and coworkers.
>
> They weren't tears of joy.

Phil Vischer, *Me, Myself, & Bob: A True Story about God, Dreams, and Talking Vegetables* viii (2006). In the next paragraph of the introduction, he describes how the entire thing was about to collapse. People were going to be laid off, and "the company and ministry [that Phil] had built in 12 years of often exasperating work was on the verge of disintegrating—

---

[8] I highly recommend this book to you. It has great insights to offer into the way creative entrepreneurs think, it presents a gripping and compelling story of the rise and fall of a closely held business, and it presents some wonderful Christian life lessons.

collapsing right before [his] eyes." *Id.* And, disintegrate it did. By September of the very next year, 2003, ChristianityToday would report that Big Idea Productions, Inc. had filed for bankruptcy and its assets had been sold to Classic Media, LLC, the company that owns Lassie and Rudolph the Red-Nosed Reindeer. Bob Smietana, *VeggieTales Creators File for Bankruptcy*, ChristianityToday (Sep. 1, 2003, 12:00 AM), http://www.christianitytoday.com/ct/2003/septemberweb-only/9-1-41.0.html.

Before we get to what went wrong, it is helpful to hear just a bit more about Mr. Vischer's dream. He wanted to build a top four family media brand (which would be in the realm of the size of Disney, Viacom, and Time Warner) that would deliver wholesome, Christian-based content that would benefit children and families. Vischer, *supra*, at 138-146. To paraphrase Larry the Cucumber, "it's for the kids."

As the above points out, Mr. Vischer's dream was well on its way to becoming a reality. After struggling to get started as most business start-ups do, VeggieTales sold some 6.2 million videos in 1998 alone. *Id.* at 147. VeggieTales videos completely dominated the Christian videos charts as early as 1997. *See, e.g., id.* at 127. Further, in 1997, Gaylord Entertainment wanted to buy Big Idea for $12 million. *Id.* at 128-129. Big Idea had truly seen explosive growth, and that is in part what killed the company—poorly managed growth.

Many companies die in the early years of their existence, not from no growth, but from too much growth that is poorly managed. This is one of the things that did Big Idea in. *Id.* at 158-160. Accordingly, better business management skills would have saved Big Idea.

Legal professionals sometimes find themselves helping clients with business management and accounting-type issues, so this is certainly relevant. However, even more relevant to this book, is the fact that Big Idea was also done in by some very poor legal advice. Obviously, this case is an example. It is not clear whether Big Idea's attorneys were ever involved in the negotiations over the licensing agreement with Lyrick, but no lawyer should encourage clients to enter into such huge and important business relationships without "getting it in writing." Further, Big Idea's lawyer did offer some other legal advice that was not good, such as taking on an unbeliever as a shareholder in order to raise money during the early years (which arguably violates 2 *Cor.* 6:14-18.) *Id.* at 105, 148.

Accordingly, better legal representation could have really helped Big Idea succeed. It could have possibly prevented this Christian entertainment company from having to sell itself to a non-Christian company. It could have prevented a costly bankruptcy, and the loss of a dream. We are all called to be good stewards of the time, talents, and treasure—everything really—that God has entrusted to us. An important way that a legal professional can do that is by providing good legal representation that helps others to do that.

What's the end of the story? After the above case reversed the District Court's ruling, the additional money freed up paid all of Big Idea's creditors that had not been paid in the earlier bankruptcy. However, of course, by then it was too late for Mr. Vischer to get the company back. It was already sold and that could not be undone. *Id.* at 259-260. VeggieTales has changed hands a few times since the bankruptcy sale, but the long and short of it is that someone else owns and operates Mr. Vischer's dream. It will be operated consistently with his vision for it only to the extent that this vision makes money. The market, not Christian principles, is now the sole guiding force.

CHAPTER 6
IS THERE A MORAL OBLIGATION TO PERFORM CONTRACTS?

Throughout this book, we have assumed that a moral obligation exists to keep one's word. We have assumed that there is a certain sacredness about promises in general and contracts in particular and that they should therefore be fulfilled. Obviously, the Bible clearly teaches that promises should be kept in a number of verses. *See, e.g., Exodus* 20:16, *Leviticus* 19:11, *Psalm* 15:1-4 and 58:3, *Proverbs* 6:16-19, *Ecclesiastes* 5:4-7, *Matthew* 5:33-37, *Ephesians* 4:25, and *Colossians* 3:9. Further, it seems that virtually every child at a very young age assumes that promises made to them should be kept. As a father of seven, I have had one of my children say to another on many occasions—"hey, you promised!"[1]

Given the ubiquity of the idea that there is generally some level of moral obligation to keep one's word, you might think that all legal scholars and jurisprudes work under those same assumptions that we have made throughout this book. After all, even children live and work under these assumptions. However, you would be wrong. In fact, the most influential jurisprudential thought system in America today rejects the so-called moral theory of contract law (the one we have been working under) in favor of what they refer to as the option theory of contract law. That thought system is typically referred to as law and economics.

Before we consider the option theory of contract law, and it logical outworking—efficient breach, we should first consider law and economics a bit in order to have a better understanding of the approach to law that leads to the adoption of option theory of contract law. As previously stated, law and economics is the most influential jurisprudential thought

---

[1] Of course, children are born with a sin nature in addition to some understanding of God's requirements. *See Romans* 1:18-3:18. Therefore, just like us, they are quick to hold others to the requirements of the law but slower to be willing to fulfill the law themselves. Such is the heritage we have from our father Adam—praise God we have a different one in Christ! *Romans* 5:12-21.

system of our time.   In the preface to his immensely popular and influential "textbook-treatise" on law and economics entitled *Economic Analysis of Law*, Judge Richard A. Posner asserts that law and economics "is the foremost interdisciplinary field of legal studies."[2] In support of this statement, he writes:

> The former dean of the Yale Law School, a critic of the law and economics movement, nevertheless has called it "an enormous enlivening force in American legal thought" and says that it "continues and remains the single most influential jurisprudential school in this country." More recently we read that "there is no dispute that law and economics has long been, and continues to be, the dominant theoretical paradigm for understanding and assessing law and policy."[3]

Further, Brian Bix accurately notes the enormous influence of law and economics on the American legal system. He writes:

> In the United States, no approach to law in recent decades has been more influential than the economic analysis of law (also known by the shorthand, "law and economics"); it dominates thinking about antitrust law, tort law, and most commercial law areas. Even areas which would seem uncongenial to economic analysis . . . have had significant contributions from attempts to apply this approach. There seem to be no domains free from attempts to apply this approach.[4]

Bix continues:

> The current influence of law and economics can be seen in the way that even those highly critical of that approach use its terminology and respond to the issues it raises. There is a sense in which law and economics now sets the agenda, or at least offers the initial framework, for most

---

[2] Richard A. Posner, *Economic Analysis of Law* xxi (8th ed. 2011).

[3] *Id.* (footnotes omitted) (citing and quoting Anthony T. Kronman, *Remarks at the Second Driker Forum for Excellence in the Law*, 42 Wayne L. Rev. 115, 144 and 160 (1995) and Jon Hanson and David Yosifson, *The Situation: An Introduction to the Situational Character, Critical Realism, Power Economics, and Deep Capture*, 152 U. Pa. L. Rev. 129, 142 (2003)).

[4] Brian Bix, *Jurisprudence: Theory and Context* 201 (5th ed. 2009).

discussions of policy and reform in American academic, legal, and political debate.[5]

Obviously, such an influential thought system is one that Christian legal professionals must understand and to which we must be able to make a response.

In part, law and economics has become so influential and widely accepted in our times because it seeks to avoid what Judge Posner, its leading proponent and thinker, would call "controversial metaphysical commitments."[6] For example, my belief that Jesus Christ is the sovereign Lord of the universe and that He can, by right, demand the obedience of every person and every nation on earth is definitely a controversial metaphysical commitment, according to Judge Posner.[7] As a derivative of this belief, I also believe that Jesus Christ's revelation of His righteous standards is binding on all people in all places throughout all time. Of course, this is another controversial metaphysical commitment. It is a belief that there are answers to the "big questions" (metaphysical questions) in life, such as: Is there a God? Why am I here? Is there life after death? Is the law real in some sense? Does a law above the law exist?

To be fair to Judge Posner, it is not that he just simply denies these things. Of course he does deny them—but, more tellingly, he thinks that these questions either have no answers or, if they do have answers, we can't know them and the questions themselves are not all that interesting. But, beyond simply denying them or arguing over them, law and economics scholars like Judge Posner assert that these questions and their possible answers should not be a part of the legal discourse at all. Instead, they argue that the legal system should be neutral, secular, and free from the bias and conflict that they would say comes from these controversial metaphysical commitments.

The problem is that neutrality like this is a farce. Just like me, you, dear reader, and everyone else, Judge Posner operates out of his own metaphysical commitments, or we might say he operates out of his own worldview. In fact, it is impossible not to. We all see and understand the world through a particular set of assumptions about what is true and not true about the nature of things. In other words, it is impossible to be

---

[5] *Id.*, at 202.

[6] Richard A. Posner, *The Problematics of Moral and Legal Theory* 15 (1999). For more on Judge Posner's views on this topic and some response of my own, *see* Rodney D. Chrisman, *Why I can't conceivably influence the modern secular courts, at least according to Judge Posner.*, www.RodneyChrisman.com (Jan. 13, 2011), http://www.rodneychrisman.com/2011/01/13/why-i-cant-conceivably-influence-the-modern-secular-courts-at-least-according-to-judge-posner/.

[7] *Supra*, note 6.

neutral. Finally, neutrality in law is no more possible than neutrality is in any other part of life.

Rejecting the purported neutrality in education, Dr. R. J. Rushdoony's thoughts are very helpful on this issue of neutrality. He writes:

> The idea of neutrality is, however, a myth. Every person and institution has a perspective and a plan which involves a commitment. If God is indeed the Creator of heaven and earth, and if the God of Scripture is the living God, to eliminate Him from education is not neutrality but enmity; the most important consideration of all is not considered. No man can be neutral towards God. The idea of neutrality presupposes an objectivity on the part of man which is not tenable. Moreover, we cannot assume that neutrality is essential to establishing truth; if a man is neutral towards all things, then all things are equally meaningless to him. Not even God professes to be neutral; He speaks of *hating* certain things and persons (e.g., Prov. 6:16–19). . . . Courts of law are not neutral; in a murder trial, neither the court nor the law is neutral about murder. Rather, the quest is for *justice* in procedure and judgment, something very different from neutrality.[8]

Further, noting that Cornelius Van Til denied the concept of neutrality, Dr. Rushdoony wrote "There are no neutral facts, no neutral thoughts, no neutral man nor reason. All men, facts, and thinking either begin with the sovereign and triune God, or they begin with rebellion against Him."[9]

Neutrality being impossible, and everything either being in submission to God or in rebellion against Him (remember it was Jesus who said "he that is not with me is against me" in *Matthew* 12:30,) points to the reality that everything, including law, is at its base religious and theological.[10] Applying this to law, Dr. Rushdoony wrote:

> Law is in every culture *religious in origin*. Because law governs man and society, because it establishes and declares the meaning of justice and righteousness, law is inescapably religious, in that it establishes in practical

---

[8] R. J. Rushdoony, *Sovereignty* 225–226 (2007) (emphasis in original).

[9] R. J. Rushdoony, *Systematic Theology in Two Volumes: Volume I* 60 (1994).

[10] *See, e.g.,* Rodney D. Chrisman, *The Law is Inescapably Theological (Just Like the Rest of Life)*, www.RodneyChrisman.com (August 13, 2010), http://www.rodneychrisman.com/2010/08/13/the-law-is-inescapably-theological-just-like-the-rest-of-life/.

fashion the ultimate concerns of a culture. Accordingly, a fundamental and necessary premise in any and every study of law must be, *first*, a recognition of this religious nature of law.

Second, it must be recognized that in any culture *the source of law is the god of that society.* If law has its source in man's reason, then reason is the god of that society. If the source is an oligarchy, or in a court, senate, or ruler, then that source is the god of that system. Thus, in Greek culture law was essentially a religiously humanistic concept.

. . .

Modern humanism, the religion of the state, locates law in the state and thus makes the state, or the people as they find expression in the state, the god of the system. As Mao Tse-Tung has said, "Our God is none other than the masses of the Chinese people." In Western culture, law has steadily moved away from God to the people (or the state) as its source, although the historic power and vitality of the West has been in Biblical faith and law.[11]

The God of our legal system used to be the God of the Bible. Now, unfortunately, it is the state or the civil magistrate, and this transition has been cloaked in a claim of neutrality cleverly designed to drive all viewpoints except the secular humanist out of the law and out of the public square.

Judge Posner and other law and economics scholars, operating from a position of supposed and self-declared neutrality, posit that economic analysis, instead of a moral standard ultimately anchored in the God of the Bible, should be the guiding principle for law and policy in America. Further, they argue that this is really what judges have been doing all along anyway—seeking economic efficiency in order to increase societal wealth. In fact, according to law and economics, the goal of the legal system should be to facilitate (and not unnecessarily impede) the flow of societal resources to those users who value them most thereby maximizing and increasing societal wealth. The best way to accomplish this is generally considered to be through the market.

This is a very appealing proposition. After all, can't we all agree that society being wealthier is a good thing? Isn't it a worthy goal to find some guiding principle around which we can all "just get along?" Perhaps, but we have to remember the earlier discussion about law being inexorably tied to religion and theology.

---

[11] R. J. Rushdoony, *The Institutes of Biblical Law, Volume One* 4-5 (1973) (quoting Mao Tse-Tung, *The Foolish Old Man Who Removed Mountains* 3 (1966)) (emphasis in original).

Conservative Christians may often find themselves in agreement with law and economics scholars on many issues. However, we should avoid being seduced by this. When we agree, we often agree for very, very different reasons. We may agree on some particular fact, but the principles that lead us to this conclusion are far from one another. For example, many conservative Christians agree that the market is a good thing and that we do want resources in the hands of people who will use them most efficiently, just like many law and economics scholars. However, we don't reach this conclusion because we believe that the maximization of societal wealth is the greatest good and should be the guiding principle of law and policy. Rather, we reach this conclusion because God, as the Creator of the world, chose to entrust all of His creation to mankind, and we are therefore stewards with a duty to manage everything that God has entrusted to us in an efficient and non-wasteful manner. Some of the conclusions are the same, but the ultimate principles are very different.[12]

One area where the conclusion and the ultimate principle are both different is in the area of performance and breach, and this brings us back to the topic with which we began the chapter. Law and economics scholars view the greatest good that the legal system should be seeking as economic efficiency. They don't see a place for moral theory or talk of moral obligations in the law, as many Americans would assume. Accordingly, they view contracts as merely options, not as moral obligations. Therefore, they conclude that, when it is efficient to do so, one should break his word and breach his contract and just pay damages. Judge Posner describes it this way:

> Many students of contract law believe that because a contract is a promise, breaking a contract, at least if it is done deliberately (remember that many breaches of contract are involuntary), is a wrongful act. Those who hold this view are apt to think that the remedies for breach of contract are inadequate.
>
> But is it a sound view? Oliver Wendell Holmes argued, in the spirit of positive economics, that contracts are options—when you sign a contract in which you promise a specified performance (supplying a product or providing a service), you buy an option to perform or pay damages. . . . As long as you pay the damages awarded by the court in the promisee's suit for breach of contract, whether they are specified in the clause or computed according to the

---

[12] For an interesting critique of law and economics by a Christian economics professor who teaches at the University of Virginia, *see* Kenneth G. Elzinga, *Law and Economics: Is there a Higher Law?*, 36 Pepp. L. Rev. 507 (2009).

principles of contract damages, no blame can attach to your not performing, even if it was deliberate—even if, for example, you did not perform simply because someone offered you more money for the product or service that you had undertaken to supply in the contract, and you lacked the capacity to supply both the promisee and the new, more necessitous customer. You have not really broken your promise, because what you promised (though that is not how the contract will have been worded) was either-or: not performance but either performance or compensation for the cost of nonperformance to the other party to the contract.

The option theory is thus a "no-fault" theory of contract law.[13]

As the foregoing demonstrates, law and economics posits a "no-fault" theory of contract law that makes it so no one is ever guilty of breaking his word by breaching a contract. The contract may be written that way, but in fact it does not say what it means. What it really means is an option—perform or pay damages. Morality and fulfilling commitments has nothing to do with it, at least according to Judge Posner.

Christians, and indeed most scholars throughout the history of the Western legal tradition, have reached a different conclusion working from an entirely different premise. Working from a premise that there is a moral obligation to keep one's word and that this moral obligation is relevant to contract law, Christian scholars reach a conclusion very different from Posner's. Prof. Bern's analysis from his exceptional *Biblical Model* article cited earlier in this book is excellent example of Christian thinking on this topic.

> *A* promises to purchase raw materials for use in his manufacturing business from *B* for a price, and *B* promises in return to sell them to *A* at that price. Thereafter, and before *A* has changed his position in reliance on the promise, *B* breaks his promise to *A* and sells them at a higher price to *C*. *A* sues, requesting appropriate relief for the breach.

---

[13] Posner, *Economic Analysis*, *supra* note 2, at 170 (quoting Oliver W. Holmes, *The Path of the Law*, 10 Harv. L. Rev. 457, 462 (1897). Oliver W. Holmes has a near semi-divine status in American jurisprudence, but most Americans even today would find his worldview disturbing. For more on Justice Holmes and his worldview, *see* Rodney D. Chrisman, *Holmes the Monster*, www.RodneyChrisman.com (January 28, 2011), http://www.rodneychrisman.com/2011/01/28/holmes-the-monster/.

Under the Biblical Model analysis, *B's* conduct of breaking his promise under these circumstances would, at the very least, appear to be sin for which he is accountable to God. That fact alone, however, serious as it is, does not mean that the breach is within the jurisdiction of Civil Government. The additional inquiry must be made as to whether *B's* conduct in this instance is such as to put him in the category of an evildoer with respect to which Civil Government has jurisdiction to act.

In pursuing that inquiry, recall that under the stewardship-dominion mandate *A* is under a duty to steward to the glory of God all of his time, talent and resources. *B* is under a duty to God to recognize that duty and not to interfere with *A's* carrying it out. By his words of promise, *B* created an expectation in *A* that his assistance in *A's* stewardship-dominion activity would be forthcoming and has now dashed that expectation. Not only has *A's* expectation been disappointed, but the transaction costs (including time, effort, and potential foregone opportunities) inherent in putting the *A-B* agreement together have been wasted. Additional transaction costs will be incurred when *A* arranges a substitute transaction or otherwise alters his business operations to accommodate not having the raw materials, to say nothing of the transaction costs in endeavoring to obtain redress from *B* for the disruption he has caused. These adverse effects confirm that *B's* actions have interfered with *A's* efforts to carry out his stewardship-dominion duties to God and constitute evildoing (*kakos*) with respect to which Civil Government has jurisdiction. Additionally, such actions, if unchecked by Civil Government, also threaten the sanctity of promise and its continued effectiveness as a unique vehicle for enhancing stewardship-dominion capabilities.

This position is, of course, contrary to that of the proponents of law and economics analysis who advocate the "efficient breach" theory. The premise for such analysis is the non-Biblical proposition that the greatest good is achieved by actions which facilitate the movement of goods and services to their highest and best use, judged by the willingness, at a particular point in time, of people to pay for them. According to that analysis, because *C* is willing to pay more for the materials now than *A* had previously agreed to pay, *B* should break his promise to *A* and sell them to *C* if, after *B* pays *A's* damages, *B* will have a larger profit and the materials will be in the hands of the one who presumably has a more valuable use for them.

Apart from its non-Biblical premise, which undermines the planning benefit that is one of the key individual and societal gains from agreement, the efficient breach theory is patently deficient in other respects.[14]

Prof. Bern then goes on to explain at least four reasons why the efficient breach theory is a bad idea, beyond its undermining the sanctity of promise and its non-biblical premise. They are: (1) Efficient breach theory is deficient, even under its own premises, in that "it does not attempt to measure all of the costs inherent in the transaction in determining whether the overall wealth of society is increased or decreased by the breach."[15]   (2) "[E]fficient breach theory ignores the reality that the remedies system, pursuant to which *A*'s damages will be measured, is grossly undercompensatory."[16]   (3)"[T]he instances in which an 'efficient breach' can occur are most limited. They occur only in instances of market distortion such that *C* is willing to pay greater than market price for the materials."[17]   (4) "[E]ven if one were to accept the premise that society will be better off if the materials in the Illustration end up in *C*'s hands, there are ways to accomplish that other than by *B*'s breach."[18]

NOTES AND QUESTIONS

1. What Do You Think? Do you find yourself more in agreement with Prof. Bern or Judge Posner? Should we really attempt to understand the law apart from any moral standards? Can we? What do you think?

_____

_____

_____

_____

_____

---

[14] Roger Bern, *A Biblical Model for Analysis of Issues of Law and Public Policy: With Illustrative Applications to Contracts, Antitrust, Remedies and Public Policy Issues,* 6 Regent U. L. Rev. 103, 132-34 (1995) (citations omitted).

[15] *Id.* at 134.

[16] *Id.* Prof. Bern writes more on remedies in this article at pages 159-173.

[17] *Id.* at 134-135.

[18] *Id.* at 135.

2. Performance or Damages, Which Would You Prefer? Let's imagine you engage in a common Internet commerce transaction such as buying an item on eBay. Do you view the contract that is made when you win the bid as being an option? In other words, do you understand the transaction that you just entered into to be such that the other party can either send you the item as agreed or just choose not to and pay the damages to you? Would you be just as satisfied with the damages? Would you think that the other person had wronged you if he broke his word and didn't ship the item?

If efficient breach theory is correct, and contracts really are just options, then it seems that you should be indifferent as between the outcomes above. You should be equally satisfied with performance or damages. However, most people probably don't feel that way. Further, if this idea were to become widespread, it would undermine the trust that is necessary for commercial activity.

Think about it for a moment. When we order things online from Amazon.com or Ebay, we are placing a significant amount of trust in these companies and the sellers (if it is a different party.) This trust makes it very efficient for people to enter into these types of transactions, and, as Prof. Bern points out, voluntary agreements are very useful in helping us to fulfill the stewardship-dominion mandate. This trust exists, in part, because there is a widely recognized moral obligation to keep one's word. Accordingly, undermining that trust by eroding the moral obligation at its foundation would eventually have serious consequences for commercial activity and, contra the law and economics position, would actually make everyone worse off.

_____

_____

_____

_____

_____

3. Damages Inadequate? Prof. Bern thinks that contract damages and remedies are inadequate. Judge Posner seems to disagree. What do you think? Are they inadequate? If so, what should they be?

_____

_____

_____

_____

Chapter 7
Is Commercial Activity a Good Thing?

Introduction to the Uniform Commercial Code

In this chapter, we will begin our study of the Uniform Commercial Code (often called the "UCC.") Our studies will take us through two articles from the UCC, UCC Articles 2 and 2A dealing with sales and leases of goods. This week considers the formation and terms of these special contracts, and next week considers performance and remedies. Accordingly, it may be helpful to begin with a discussion of the nature of the UCC and its comparison to what we studied in the course up to this point—common law contract law.

The UCC is probably the most successful uniform law project ever. It has been adopted into law in all 50 states, the District of Columbia, and various other U.S. territories, etc. It is relatively uniform, although each jurisdiction has adopted non-uniform amendments and not all of the jurisdictions have adopted the same versions. The UCC is designed to make the law of commercial activity relatively uniform across the several jurisdictions in the United States. The way it works is by providing what you might call an overlay on common law contract law, which can vary considerably from state to state. The idea is this, anywhere the UCC speaks it trumps common law contract law. To put it another way, it supersedes common law contract law in the extent it deals with a topic. However, to the extent that there are gaps in the UCC, one looks to common law contract law to fill those gaps.

You could imagine it like a catcher and a backstop. When a pitcher throws, the catcher will often be the one to catch the ball (assuming, of course, that the batter does not hit it.) The catcher is the UCC. However, if the ball gets past the catcher, it will be caught by the backstop, which in our analogy is common law contract law. Both work together. We look first to the UCC in areas where it governs, and then, if it does not speak to a particular issue, we look to the principles of the common law contract law.

Goodness of Commercial Activity

Throughout our studies so far, we have generally assumed that just contracts and just commercial activity are good things. Therefore, we would think that the law should provide a framework that generally encourages and facilitates this type of just activity, while discouraging unjust activity in this area, in order to facilitate people in fulfilling their stewardship-dominion mandate. But, is this true? Is commercial activity a good thing? The following excerpted article should help you consider this important question.[1]

Rodney D. Chrisman, *Can a Merchant Please God?: The Church's Historic Teaching on the Goodness of Just Commercial Activity as a Foundational Principle of Commercial Law Jurisprudence*
6 Liberty U. L. Rev. 453 (2012)

I. Introduction

Can a merchant please God? To modern readers that question undoubtedly seems unusual. Perhaps some are offended by such a question, feeling that it is intolerant and should not even be asked in public discourse.[2] Others might view it as an example of a quaint concern

---

[1] Editor's Note: In the following article, many footnotes have been omitted, but others have been retained. For convenience sake, where they have been retained, there original numbering has not been retained. If you would like to see the entire article with all of the footnotes as they appear in the original, you may visit http://www.rodneychrisman.com/articles/ for a copy.

[2] Such people would likely see theology, or perhaps the preferred term now is spirituality, as a purely private matter that has no part in the public discourse. While to many this may seem natural and the way things have always been, it is, in fact, a very recent and unfortunate development. Of this development, Professor Berman writes that

> the significant factor in this regard—in the nineteenth century and even more in the twentieth—was the very gradual reduction of traditional religion to the level of a personal, private matter, without public influence on legal development, while other belief systems—new secular religions (ideologies, "isms")—were raised to the level of passionate faiths for which people collectively were willing not only to die but also to live new lives.

HAROLD J. BERMAN, LAW AND REVOLUTION: THE FORMATION OF THE WESTERN LEGAL TRADITION 31 (1983).

from a bygone era when God was believed to exist and therefore His opinion of things seemed quite important. Persons holding to this view might well consider this question to be entirely irrelevant.[3] Perhaps others still view a question like this as very important for their personal lives as they desire to please God with all they do.[4] These persons could be said to view this question, and others like it, to be of great spiritual importance. However, very few people indeed would imagine that such a question might be of grave *legal* importance, in addition to any spiritual significance it might have.[5]

---

[3] There is likely a range of opinions in this group. Some would say it is irrelevant to them, but it could be relevant for an individual who views such things as important in his own private life. Oftentimes, they would also consider it to be entirely irrelevant and even inappropriate to ask such a question in the public square or to make it a part of a policy consideration. Some in this category view any kind of religious thought, such as this, as a mere crutch for those who need such things to deal with life. This author was at one point an atheist, and he, at that time, viewed religion in this manner.

Finally, there are others, such as Christopher Hitchens (recently deceased), Richard Dawkins, and others among the so-called "new atheists," who are much more militant to such views. These men view the belief in God as something that is positively dangerous for society. Therefore, they would likely label the question "can a merchant please God?" as one that is destructive even to consider. *See, e.g.*, CHRISTOPHER HITCHENS, GOD IS NOT GREAT: HOW RELIGION POISONS EVERYTHING (2007) ("The human invention of god is the problem to begin with."); RICHARD DAWKINS, THE GOD DELUSION 348 (2006) ("Faith can be very very dangerous, and deliberately to implant it into the vulnerable mind of an innocent child is a grievous wrong.").

[4] Modern evangelicals, conservative Catholics, and others would fall within this category. As a conservative evangelical, this author would fall into this category as he hopes to do everything that he does for the glory of God, and he does believe that God exists and finds His opinion to be the most important one in the universe.

The Westminster Shorter Catechism would reflect this view in its very first question, which asks, "What is the chief end of man?" The answer given is that "[m]an's chief end is to glorify God, and to enjoy him for ever [sic]." Westminster Assembly, *The Westminster Shorter Catechism, in* WESTMINSTER CONFESSION OF FAITH 287 (Free Presbyterian Publications 1994) (1646). Further, the biblical support for this position is voluminous. *See, e.g.*, 1 *Corinthians* 10:31 ("Whether, then, you eat or drink or whatever you do, do all to the glory of God.") (New American Standard Bible: Updated Edition (hereinafter all Scripture quotations are taken from the New American Standard Bible: Updated Edition, unless otherwise specifically noted)); *Colossians* 3:23-24 ("Whatever you do, do your work heartily, as for the Lord rather than for men, knowing that from the Lord you will receive the reward of the inheritance. It is the Lord Christ whom you serve.").

[5] The author also falls into this small minority of people who believe that the teachings of the Bible are highly relevant for all of life, including any legal system. While this represents a minority view now, it was once assumed across virtually all of Western Civilization. *See, e.g.*, BERMAN, *supra* note [2] at 115 ("All these laws were considered to be subordinate to the precepts contained in the Bible (both the Old and New Testaments) and in the writings of the early church fathers . . . ."); STEPHEN D. SMITH, LAW'S QUANDARY 45-48 (2004); *see generally,* Stuart Banner, *When Christianity was Part of the Common Law*, 16 LAW & HIST. REV. 27 (1998).

Yet, the issue of whether a merchant can please God was one of paramount importance to jurists and theologians, not to mention merchants, during the high middle ages. This question was central to the consideration of commercial law during the period when the Western legal tradition, Western commercial law, and the institutions therein, were being formed.[6] The answer to this theological question impacted the development of the Law Merchant and therefore ultimately still impacts Western commercial law to this day.[7] Accordingly, this Article considers how the answer to this question was resolved during that time and suggests that perhaps this understanding could form the foundation for understanding the jurisprudence of commercial law today.

If so, this would be a welcome development for there is much confusion as to the purpose, concept, or jurisprudence of commercial law.[8]

---

[6] BERMAN, *supra* note [2], at 336-39 (addressing the issue of commercial law and theology in particular, and the book as a whole discusses the formation of the Western legal tradition). This book won the 1984 SCRIBES Book Award awarded by the American Bar Association for the best new book on a legal subject. Professor Berman had a long and distinguished career as a Professor of Law at Harvard Law School and Emory University School of Law.

In this excellent work, Professor Berman persuasively argues that the Western legal tradition was formed during the eleventh and twelfth centuries. Professor Berman refers to this period, which is often referred to as the Gregorian Reforms under Pope Gregory VII, as "the Papal Revolution of 1075-1122." *Id.* at 19. He uses the word "revolution . . . to refer to . . . epoch-making periods" such as the Protestant Reformation and the American and French Revolutions. *Id.* at 19-20. His study details the immense changes in the religious, educational, societal, economic, and legal systems of Western Europe during this period that led to the formation of the Western legal tradition. One of those changes was a shift in the church's attitude toward merchants and commercial activity, which serves as the topic of this article. The author is persuaded by Professor Berman's work, and therefore, this work proceeds under the assumption that the Western legal tradition was formed during the Papal Revolution, and the term "Papal Revolution" is therefore borrowed and used herein to refer to this period for the sake of convenience. If the reader takes issue with this conclusion regarding the formation of the Western legal tradition, the author would respectfully direct him to Professor Berman's work. To set forth fully those arguments is well beyond the scope of this Article.

[7] This Article does not take the position that modern commercial law, and its primary manifestation in the United States of America—the Uniform Commercial Code ("UCC")—*is* the modern law merchant. That is a matter open to scholarly debate and discussion. *See, e.g.,* Jim C. Chen, *Code, Custom, and Contract: The Uniform Commercial Code as Law Merchant,* 27 TEX. INT'L L.J. 91 (1991). Rather, this Article merely makes the rather unremarkable and hopefully uncontroversial assumption that the UCC has in its lineage an ancestor known as the Law Merchant and that an understanding of the Law Merchant might help in understanding its descendants—Western commercial law in general and perhaps the UCC in particular.

[8] Professor Steven D. Smith suggests that confusion reigning in the law as a whole today comes from the abandonment of what he describes as the classical approach to law, which was very much based upon Christianity and the God of the Bible. *See* SMITH, *supra* note [5], at 45-51, 151-53, 155-57, 174-75 (2004).

[The article continues here by describing some of the modern confusion with regard to the purpose or jurisprudence of commercial law.]

Western civilization has forgotten or rejected the theology that served as the foundation for its law in general and its commercial law in particular. Without a proper understanding of commercial law's historically theological roots, it does appear that commercial law, and indeed much of the rest of Western law, lacks any satisfactory conceptual explanation.

In his excellent book *Law and Revolution: The Formation of the Western Legal Tradition*, Professor Harold J. Berman discusses this development in the Western legal tradition that has so obscured the jurisprudential foundations of not just commercial law but nearly all of Western law.

> [The] basic institutions, concepts, and values of Western legal systems have their sources in religious rituals, liturgies, and doctrines of the eleventh and twelfth centuries . . . Over the intervening centuries, these religious attitudes and assumptions have changed fundamentally, and today [in 1983] their theological sources seem to be in the process of drying up. Yet the legal institutions, concepts, and values that have derived from them still survive, often unchanged. *Western legal science is a secular theology, which often makes no sense because its theological presuppositions are no longer accepted.*
>
> . . .
>
> [T]he legal systems of all Western countries, and of all non-Western countries that have come under the influence of Western law, are *a secular residue of religious attitudes and assumptions which historically found expression first in liturgy and rituals and doctrine of the church and thereafter in institutions and concepts and values of the law. When these historical roots are not understood, many parts of the law appear to lack any underlying source of validity.*[9]

Commercial law, accordingly, appears to "make[] no sense" and "lack any underlying source of validity" because "its theological presuppositions are no longer accepted" or even understood.

Professor Steven D. Smith has also written on this confusion that pervades jurisprudence in the modern legal community in his excellent book entitled *Law's Quandary*.[10] Beyond a discussion on commercial law jurisprudence, Professor Smith exposes how all modern jurisprudential

---

[9] BERMAN, *supra* note [2], at 165-66 (emphasis added).
[10] *See* SMITH, *supra* note [5].

schools are operating in ontological gaps, i.e., their generally accepted ontological inventories are insufficient to guide, explain, or justify their views of the law.[11] Modern jurisprudence lacks the foundation that the "classical approach" had in abundance and all as a result of the worldview with which the legal scholars and theologians prior to the modern era approached law.[12] "Blackstone and Story were, after all, heirs of a worldview that assumed that God was real—*more* real than anything else, in fact, or *necessarily* rather than just *contingently* real—and had created the universe according to a providential plan."[13]

Indeed, as Professors Berman and Smith aptly point out, not only are the theological foundations of the law, to use Professor Berman's phraseology, or the classical approach to the law to use Professor Smith's, no longer accepted nor understood, they are no longer even considered as a proper knowledge base from which to draw in developing, critiquing, or understanding the law. In our post-modern world, "for the first time, religion has become largely a private affair, while law has become largely a matter of practical expediency."[14] This hearkens back to Professor Scott's lament that commercial law often appears as little more than a set of rules according to which businessmen may govern their affairs. The bankruptcy of such a view of law is obvious, and it is not surprising therefore that it does not inspire confidence or lend itself to a consistent jurisprudence.

In fact, Professor Berman notes that these changes in the way that not just commercial law but all of law is viewed have led to a crisis of confidence in the law. He writes that "[a]lmost all the nations of the West are threatened today by a cynicism about law, leading to a contempt for law."[15] Further, the alternatives offered are not up to the task of dispelling the current cynicism because they do not provide a view of the law that is consistent, comprehensive, and that corresponds to reality.[16] The only jurisprudential system that can possibly offer a consistent, comprehensive, and corresponding view of the law is the "classical

---

[11] *Id.* at 5-37, 157, 175.

[12] *Id.* at 45-48.

[13] *Id.* at 46.

[14] BERMAN, *supra* note [2], at vi.

[15] *Id.* at 40.

[16] Berman stated that

Cynicism about the law, and lawlessness, will not be overcome by adhering to a so-called realism which denies the autonomy, the integrity, and the ongoingness of our legal tradition. In the words of Edmund Burke, those who do not look backward to their ancestry will not look forward to their posterity.

Id. at 41. Further, as Professor Smith demonstrates, the various modern jurisprudential alternatives are not able to rescue law from that charge that it does not make sense. SMITH, *supra* note [5], at 65-96.

approach," or, as Dean Jeff Tuomala calls it, "law of nature" jurisprudence.[17]

Unfortunately, as Professors Berman and Smith point out, this view of the law is generally considered to be an inappropriate basis for public discourse or academic argumentation. Professor Berman laments that religion has been relegated to a purely private role, and Professor Smith notes that the religious ontology, though possibly able to rescue the law from its present quandary, is intellectually unacceptable due to "[t]he taken-for-granted 'fact' of [inevitable] secularization."[18] Professor Smith notes that the clear result of this "inevitable secularization" has been

> that academics have internalized a norm prescribing that religious beliefs are inadmissible *in academic explanations.* Historians may believe in God, but they do not explain historical events by reference to the workings of God in history (as was once common). Scientists may be religious believers, and they may even argue that science provides support for religious belief, but they typically do not resort to religious explanations for specific natural phenomena in the way that even "Enlightened" thinkers like Jefferson once did. With respect to the legal academy, Laycock himself draws this conclusion: "One inference is that the believers feel obliged to be quiet about [their beliefs]" in an academic context.[19]

This article endeavors to violate this norm by looking to the classical approach to law in order to begin to develop a consistent, comprehensive, and corresponding view of commercial law.

That said, a fully developed and thorough-going jurisprudence of commercial law is beyond this single work. Instead, the goal of this article is to take a look at the historical theological developments surrounding the birth of commercial law within the Western legal tradition. By considering the theological issues that surrounded commercial law at this formulatory state of the Western legal tradition, it is hoped that a better

---

[17] *See, e.g.,* SMITH, *supra* note [5], at 151-53, where Professor Smith notes that the classical approach might be able to rescue us from our current "quandary," but then laments that

> [w]e are by now far removed, of course, from times in which such an account could be presented openly and discussed respectfully. For many of us, the classical account is a distant memory; for others it is not even that. So perhaps all we can confidently say is that the classical account, if it were admissible and believable, *might* be of some help.

Id. at 151-52.

[18] *Id.* at 35.

[19] *Id.* at 36 (alteration in original) (footnotes omitted).

view of the overarching purpose of commercial law can be seen. Such a purpose, while not establishing a thorough-going jurisprudence of commercial law, has promise to prove most helpful in the goal of beginning to develop one. In order to accomplish this goal, this article employs the classical approach to law. In order to do that, it considers the church's historic answer to the question with which this paper began—"can a merchant please God?"

II. Can a Merchant Please God?: The Church's Teachings Prior to the Papal Revolution

"Can a merchant please God?" This question had enormous spiritual implications for the people of Western Christendom in the medieval period. The people of the middle ages were consumed with the question that the Philippian jailor asked Paul and Silas, "What must I do to be saved?"[20] Hell and purgatory seemed very real in those days, and the issue of how to avoid the eternal punishment of God was on the order of first importance in nearly everyone's mind. Thus, it was critically important to a merchant, and indeed the jurists and theologians, of the time to answer the question whether a merchant can ever be pleasing to God.

Further, the medieval period knew nothing of the modern idea of the "separation of church and state," which to most modern elites means

---

[20] This question arose from an incident in what is commonly referred to as Paul's second missionary journey. Paul and Silas were ministering in Philippi in Macedonia. Paul cast a demonic spirit out of a slave girl whose masters had been profiting from the spirit's purported ability to tell the future through the girl. Upon seeing that they could no longer profit in this way, her masters stirred up the crowd against Paul and Silas. *See Acts* 16:11-21. Luke writes:

> The crowd rose up together against them, and the chief magistrates tore their robes off them and proceeded to order them to be beaten with rods. When they had struck them with many blows, they threw them into prison, commanding the jailer to guard them securely; and he, having received such a command, threw them into the inner prison and fastened their feet in the stocks.
>
> But about midnight Paul and Silas were praying and singing hymns of praise to God, and the prisoners were listening to them; and suddenly there came a great earthquake, so that the foundations of the prison house were shaken; and immediately all the doors were opened and everyone's chains were unfastened. When the jailer awoke and saw the prison doors opened, he drew his sword and was about to kill himself, supposing that the prisoners had escaped. But Paul cried out with a loud voice, saying, "Do not harm yourself, for we are all here!" And he called for lights and rushed in, and trembling with fear he fell down before Paul and Silas, and after he brought them out, he said, "Sirs, what must I do to be saved?"

Acts 16:22–30. Paul and Silas answered, "'Believe in the Lord Jesus, and you will saved, you and your household.'" *Acts* 16:31.

something more along the lines of the "separation of religion and state."[21] Rather, in the medieval period, when the Western legal tradition was born, and indeed throughout most of its history, there has existed an integral connection between law and theology, religion and state. Indeed, during this time, law developed under the influence of theology.[22] Most relevant to this paper, Professor Berman asserts that the Law Merchant,[23] which had its origins during the time of the Papal Revolution, developed under the influence of the church's teachings on commercial transactions. He writes:

> From the point of view of the Christian social theory which prevailed in the formative period of Western commercial institutions, the economic activities of merchants, like other secular activities, were no longer to be considered as necessarily "a danger to salvation"; on the contrary, they were considered to be a path to salvation, if carried on according to the principles laid down by the church. These principles were spelled out in the canon law. From the church's point of view, the law developed by the merchants to regulate their own interrelationships, the *lex mercatoria*, was supposed to reflect, not contradict, the canon law. The merchants did not always agree with that. *They did not disagree, however, that the salvation of their souls depended on the conformity of their practices to a system of law based on the will of God as manifested in reason and conscience.*
>
> Thus the social and economic activity of merchants was not left outside the reach of moral issues. *A social and economic morality was developed which purported to guide the souls of merchants toward salvation. And that morality was embodied in law. Law was a bridge between mercantile activity and the salvation of the soul.*[24]

Thus, according to Professor Berman, the Law Merchant, the ancestor to modern commercial law, developed in light of the church's teachings on commercial activity during a time in which the worldview of Western Civilization was undeniably Christian. As stated, the law governing merchants and commercial activity was designed as a guide to salvation.

---

[21] Such a separation is, in fact, not possible. The myth of a neutral, secular arena where religions (or worldviews) do not matter is just that—a myth. However, that myth has been used very shrewdly in our time to silence all arguments in the public square that are based upon religious conviction.

[22] And, at times, theology developed under the influence of the law.

[23] Professor Berman typically refers to the Law Merchant in his book as the Mercantile Law. *See* BERMAN, *supra* note [2], at 333.

[24] *Id.* at 339 (emphasis added).

The Law Merchant helped to answer, in large part, the burning question in the mind of the merchant—"what must I do to be saved?" "Law was a bridge between mercantile activity and the salvation of the soul."[25]

The preface to Johannes Nider's work *On the Contracts of Merchants* bears out Professor Berman's comments. The purpose of his work, according to Friar Nider, an "expert physician[] of souls," is to "separate what is just from what is unjust" in the dealings of merchants, such that rules can be determined "according to which it can be seen in some way or other when merchants may be more or less secure in their" commercial activity.[26] As the editor of the English translation of *On the Contracts of Merchants* rightly notes, Nider's "references to that which is 'just' . . . should be read as intended primarily to remind the reader that worldly action should be judged by churchly standards of morality."[27] Such a work as Nider's would have been respected in a time when the prevailing "social theory" was dominated by the Christian worldview, as was clearly the case in the Middle Ages. The preceding quote by Professor Berman demonstrates this to be the case. "The merchants did not always agree" that the Law Merchant should reflect the canon law, but they did agree "that the salvation of their souls depended on the conformity of their practices to a system of law based on the will of God."[28] Further, there was no doubt that, during the time of the formation of the Western legal tradition, the law was viewed as a "bridge" or "guide" for the "salvation of the soul."[29]

The dilemma for the merchant, and the theologian or jurist, concerned with such things prior to, and at the beginning of, the Papal Revolution was that the church's teachings on commercial activity prior to that time were decidedly negative. The church generally answered the question "can a merchant please God" with a resounding "no." Many modern commentators assume, correctly in part, that the teachings of the church prior to the Papal Revolution were almost entirely opposed to merchants and commercial activity. Professor Berman asserts that the church, prior to the eleventh and twelfth centuries, had evinced a

---

[25] *Id.*

[26] JOHANNES NIDER, ON THE CONTRACTS OF MERCHANTS xi (Robert B. Sherman, ed., Charles H. Reeves, trans., 1966) (circa 1430, 1468). In the introduction to ON THE CONTRACTS OF MERCHANTS, the editor writes "that Friar Nider's primary purpose for writing *De Contractibus Mercatorum* was to provide a moral guide to those" engaged in commercial activity. The guide was written "in terms of the author's understanding of the accepted views of the Roman Catholic Church of Western Europe." *Id.* at viii. ON THE CONTRACTS OF MERCHANTS is discussed in more detail herein as an example of the work of later Scholastics demonstrating their transformation of church doctrine regarding commercial activity.

[27] *Id.* at viii.

[28] BERMAN, *supra* note [2], at 339.

[29] *Id.*

universally hostile attitude toward merchants and commercial activity.[30] He quotes "the great French social and economic historian Henri Pirenne" as remarking that "'the attitude of the Church . . . towards commerce [was] not merely passive but actively hostile.'"[31] Further, Professor Berman describes the church's teachings prior to the Papal Revolution as "fundamentally opposed to the profit motive"[32] and describes the church's view of commercial activity in general as "'a danger to salvation.'"[33]

Further, Professor Gerber has described "the church's tradition [as] filled with antipathy to commerce."[34] He states that "[f]rom its inception, church tradition had painted an overwhelmingly negative picture of commercial activity."[35] Speaking of the church's "intellectual encounter with the market" in the high middle ages, he writes:

> The patristic writings that were the primary sources of authority for the church's intellectual encounter with the market were replete with denunciations of mercantile activity. Heavily influenced by Greek, especially Platonic, philosophy, these works considered commercial activity incompatible with religious salvation. A merchant could not follow the church's precepts, it was thought, because commerce required lying, deception, exploitation and other sins. Moreover, the market was seen as a threat to the Christian community, because it undermined the ideas of fairness and cohesion on which that community was based. Early medieval writers who were used as authorities during the twelfth and thirteenth centuries typically either repeated the condemnations found in patristic writings or paid little heed to commercial activity.[36]

In a footnote, Professor Gerber elaborates on the hostility patristic writers held toward commercial activity by asserting that "[t]he only patristic writer of importance during the medieval period who placed any significant emphasis on justifying commercial activity was Augustine."[37]

---

[30] BERMAN, *supra* note [2], at 336-39.

[31] *Id.* at 336 (quoting HENRI PIRENNE, ECONOMICS AND SOCIAL HISTORY OF MEDIEVAL EUROPE 48-49 (1937)).

[32] *Id.*

[33] *Id.* at 339.

[34] David J. Gerber, *Prometheus Born: The High Middle Ages and the Relationship Between Law and Economic Conduct*, 38 ST. LOUIS U. L.J. 673, 696 (1994).

[35] *Id.*

[36] *Id.* at 697 (footnotes omitted).

[37] *Id.* at 697 n.113 (citing John W. Baldwin, *The Medieval Merchant before the Bar of Canon Law*, 44 PAPERS OF THE MICHIGAN ACADEMY OF SCIENCE, ARTS AND LETTERS 287, 290 (1959)).

Cited as authority by Professor Gerber, Dr. John W. Baldwin, Professor Emeritus of History at Johns Hopkins University, wrote in *The Medieval Merchant Before the Bar of the Canon Law* that:

> The Graeco-Roman civilization of the ancient Church Fathers nourished general misgivings about the respectability of business and merchants. A cursory sampling of the obviously prominent spokesman of Greek and Roman philosophy, such as Plato, Aristotle, and Cicero, shows attitudes less than complimentary to the practical functions of the tradesman. In their own way the Church Fathers also shared in this general feeling of suspicion toward the world of commerce. The Greek Basil the Great and the Latin Jerome made bitter impassioned attacks against the accumulation of great riches. This general feeling was accompanied with specific criticisms against the merchant. Ambrose, Bishop of Milan, for example, condemned merchants for monopolistic and speculative practices that manipulated markets and robbed the public. Many of the Fathers felt that mercantile activity could hardly be kept clean of the taint of greed or *cupiditas*. In a well-known passage Tertullian condemned the profits of trading in a syllogism based on the factor of greed, "Is trading fit for the service of God?" he asked. "Certainly," was the reply, "if greed is eliminated, which is the cause of gain. But if gain is eliminated, there is no longer the need of trading." Finally the fathers were generally convinced that essentially immoral means were necessary for the merchant to succeed, that the trader must lie, cheat, deceive, and commit all manner of fraud to sell his wares.[38]

Dr. Baldwin continues by noting that Pope Leo the Great saw "buying and selling [as] morally dangerous" activities and that "those undergoing penance [should] avoid such affairs because it is difficult to buy and sell without committing sin."[39] After noting that Cassiodorus in the sixth century often made similarly anti-commercial comments, he concludes that "[o]n the whole, therefore, the Church fathers considered the merchant as *persona non grata*, and in this attitude they were merely children of their times."[40]

---

[38] John W. Baldwin, *The Medieval Merchant before the Bar of Canon Law*, 44 PAPERS OF THE MICHIGAN ACADEMY OF SCIENCE, ARTS AND LETTERS 287, 289 (1959) (footnotes omitted).

[39] *Id.* at 289-90.

[40] *Id.* at 290.

While this anti-commercial, anti-mercantile teaching undoubtedly predominated the medieval period prior to the Papal Revolution, the views represented in the preceding paragraphs of the near universal nature of these teachings among the patristics seem to overstate the case. Looking more carefully at the patristic record reveals a more nuanced view of commercial activity among the church fathers, as hinted at by Dr. Baldwin.

The church fathers were quick to condemn greed, lying, cheating, hording, monopolies, and other sins associated with money and commercial activity.[41] These condemnations often came in sermons or polemic writings—like Dr. Baldwin's quote of Tertullian above—and therefore can sometimes carry an air of hyperbole or overstatement to make a point. Polemic or sermonic discourses often lack balance because the speaker or writer is trying hard to make a point. Just as it is a rule of sound hermeneutics to read any one passage in Scripture in light of the whole counsel of scripture, it is similarly necessary to understand any one specific sermonic or polemical writing in light of the entire corpus of the work of the preacher or writer. Therefore, to fully understand the position of the patristics on commercial activity, one must consider the record as a whole, allowing for the flourishes of sermons where the balance comes only at other times and places in the speaking or writings of the subject author.

For example, Dr. Baldwin quotes Tertullian for support that the patristics viewed all trading as evil. However, in the quoted passage Tertullian is primarily concerned with the avoidance of certain trades that he considers to be subject to greed and idolatry—of which greed is a form. He does make some harsh statements against trading, such as the one that Dr. Baldwin quotes. On the other hand, he makes other statements that seem to allow for a more positive view of commerce demonstrating that his position was more nuanced. For example, after the passage that Dr. Baldwin quotes, Tertullian immediately adds, "Grant now that there be some righteousness in business, secure from the duty of watchfulness against covetousness and mendacity."[42] Further on in the same work, he says, "Let none contend that, in this way, exception may be taken to *all* trades."[43] Finally, in concluding, he states that, "No art, then, no profession, no trade, which administers either to equipping or forming idols, can be free from the title of idolatry."[44]

---

[41] *See, e.g.,* JUSTO L. GONZALEZ, FAITH AND WEALTH: A HISTORY OF EARLY CHRISTIAN IDEAS ON THE ORIGIN, SIGNIFICANCE, AND USE OF MONEY (1990).

[42] A. CLEVELAND COXE, THE ANTE-NICENE FATHERS, VOLUME III: LATIN CHRISTIANITY: ITS FOUNDER, TERTULLIAN 67 (Alexander Roberts, James Donaldson & A. Cleveland Coxe eds., 1903).

[43] *Id.* (italics in original).

[44] *Id.* at 68.

The writings of St. John Chrysostom provide another example. In a homily on *Matthew* 14:13, he condemns some trades, but not all, as evil. Speaking of the sandal-makers' trade, he says:

> And the sandal-makers' trade, so long as it makes sandals, I will not rob of the appellation of art; but when it perverts men to the gestures of women, and causes them by their sandals to grow wanton and delicate, we will set it amidst the things hurtful and superfluous, and not so much as name it an art.[45]

Chrysostom here does not condemn sandal-making or all trades, but rather indicates that he is willing to count them among the arts, which would seem to be a positive connotation. Further, his condemnation is not of the trade itself, but an abuse of the trade—the making of sandals that lead cause men to lust after the female wearers thereof. Again, this is a more nuanced position that recognizes the goodness of trading and commercial activity while also recognizing that it can be perverted to evil.

After making a much more exhaustive review of the patristic writings on money and wealth than is possible in this work, Dr. Justo L. Gonzalez concludes that:

> With respect to economic life, Ambrose stands practically alone in condemning trade, as he declares that God made the sea for fishing and not for sailing long distances in search of what the local area does not produce. Almost all other writers, however, agree that human interchange, both in goods and in other relationships, is part of the order created and intended by God. Chrysostom, in contrast with Ambrose, praises God for creating the sea so that people can travel long distances and meet each other's material needs through trade. Lactantius declares that just as God gave antlers to the deer to defend itself, humankind has been given each other, so that through social life, mutual support, and trade we may defend ourselves.[46]

This is of course nearly diametrically opposed to the positions set forth at the beginning of this section.

The explanation for this discrepancy seems to be that the Scholastics of the Papal Revolution had inherited a traditional teaching

---

[45]A SELECT LIBRARY OF THE NICENE AND POST-NICENE FATHERS OF THE CHRISTIAN CHURCH, FIRST SERIES, VOLUME X: SAINT CHRYSOSTOM: HOMILIES ON THE GOSPEL OF SAINT MATTHEW 307 (Alexander Roberts, Philip Schaff & James Donaldson eds., 1888).

[46] GONZALEZ, *supra* note [41], at 228.

that did strongly condemn commercial activity. The Scholastics, and indeed apparently many modern scholars, assumed that this teaching was held just as firmly by the patristics as it had been by those in the centuries of the middle ages preceding the Papal Revolution.[47] However, it seems more accurate to state that the patristics held a more positive view of merchants and commercial activity generally, but that the bombastic rhetorical flourishes of the patristics against the dangers relative to commerce were quickly transformed in the early middle ages into a strongly anti-commercial, anti-mercantile theology that dominated the thinking of the church until the Papal Revolution.

In addition, the Greeks and the Romans tended to have a negative view of merchants and commercial activity. Undoubtedly, this negative view did impact many of the church fathers to varying degrees. Therefore, it is possible that the writers in the early middle ages and the Scholastics (as well as many modern scholars) simply overstated the influence of Graeco-Romans on the early church fathers or conflated their beliefs with the beliefs of the patristics. Further, the theologians of the middle ages were heavily influenced by Greek and Roman thought themselves, particularly the thought of Plato, which tended to be anti-commercial in nature.[48]

While, as demonstrated in the preceding, it is somewhat of an overstatement to say that the anti-commercial teachings against which the Scholastics of the Papal Revolution reacted were characteristic of all of

---

[47] For example, the Scholastics believed that a famous church father, John Chrysostom, had written the *Opus imperfectum in Matthaeum.* (The *Opus imperfectum in Matthaeum* is an anonymous work that is discussed in much greater detail herein as the best example of the radical anti-merchant, anti-commercial teaching that came to dominate the Middle Ages prior to the Papal Revolution. For convenience sake, the *Opus imperfectum in Matthaeum* is sometimes referred to herein as simply the *Opus imperfectum.*) "The Scholastics falsely attributed [the *Opus imperfectum*] to St[.] John Chrysostom." ODD LANGHOLM, ECONOMICS IN THE MEDIEVAL SCHOOLS: WEALTH, EXCHANGE, VALUE, MONEY AND USURY ACCORDING TO THE PARIS THEOLOGICAL TRADITION 1200-1350, at 102 (1992). Professor Berman presumably follows the Scholastics in making this same mistake when he states of a quote from the *Opus imperfectum* that it "was first said by St. John Chrysostom (349-407)." BERMAN, *supra* note [2], at 618 n.5. Frederic W. Schlatter notes that "[t]he identity of the author of the *Opus imperfectum in Matthaeum* remains a vexing problem central to a problematic text" and then goes on to make a case for Annianus, a deacon from Celeda who lived and wrote during the fifth century, as the author of the text. Frederic W. Schlatter, *The Author of the* Opus Imperfectum in Matthaeum, 42 VIGILIAE CHRISTIANAE 364-75 (1988). This paper will follow the convention of referring to the author of the *Opus imperfectum* as Pseudo-Chrysostom or simply as the author.

[48] GONZALEZ, *supra* note [41], at 3-17 (discussing the various views that Greek and Roman philosophers had towards work and accumulating wealth); *see also id.* at 7 (discussing Plato's view of various commercial activities, how he "shared the negative view of trade and commerce," and how he would have forbidden buying and selling on credit).

church history prior to the eleventh and twelfth centuries, Professor Berman is certainly correct that this teaching characterized much of the medieval period immediately prior to the Papal Revolution.[49] No single source better demonstrates this hostile attitude toward merchants and commercial activity than the *Opus imperfectum in Matthaeum* ("The Incomplete Work on Matthew"). The *Opus imperfectum* is an incomplete and anonymous text believed by many scholars to have been originally written in Greek sometime in the fifth or sixth century.[50] The only extant copies of the text are in Latin.[51] The text is best described as heterodox in that it has been shown to have both Arian and Pelagian leanings.[52] Despite its heterodoxy, it was "very influential in western Europe" throughout much of the medieval period.[53] It was viewed as authoritative by the Scholastics of the Papal Revolution, and it is discussed in more detail in the next section.[54]

. . .

---

[49] BERMAN, *supra* note [2], at 336-39.

[50] ANGELIKI E. LAIOU, *Trade, Profit, and Salvation in the Late Patristic and the Byzantine Period, in* WEALTH AND POVERTY IN EARLY CHURCH AND SOCIETY, 247 (Susan R. Holman ed., 2008). However, at least one scholar has argued for Latin authorship. Schlatter, *The Author of the* Opus imperfectum in Matthaeum, 364-75.

[51] LAIOU, *supra* note [50], at 247.

[52] Frederic W. Schlatter, *The Pelagianism of the* Opus imperfectum in Matthaeum, 41 VIGILIAE CHRISTIANAE 267-85 (1987). "It has been the fate of the *Opus imperfectum in Matthaeum* since Erasmus reassessed it for his edition of 1530 to be classified as an Arian work." *Id.* at 267. Schlatter comes to the conclusion "that the *Opus imperfectum* is predominantly and basically a Pelagian work." *Id.* at 283.

[53] LAIOU, *supra* note [50], at 248.

[54] The Scholastics of the Middle Ages took Justinian's Code, the Bible, and the church fathers to be authoritative. For example, "As in the case of theology, the written text as a whole, the *Corpus Juris Civilis*, like the Bible and the writings of the church fathers, was accepted as sacred, the embodiment of reason." BERMAN, *supra* note [2], at 132. "Even apart from the universities, the church had long taught that all human law was to be tested and judged by divine law and moral law; but the university jurists added the concept of an ideal human law, the Roman law of Justinian's books, which—together with the Bible, the writings of the church fathers, the decrees of church councils and popes, and other sacred texts—provided basic legal principles and standards for criticizing and evaluating existing legal rules and institutions. These inspired writings of the past, and not what any lawgiver might say or do, provided the ultimate criteria of legality." *Id.* at 163. The use of the term "reinterpret" is therefore appropriate, although it may seem a bit odd, because this is what the Scholastics did. They did not, generally speaking, challenge the validity of the church fathers, such as the *Opus imperfectum*. Rather, they took the church fathers, along with the Bible and Justinian's Code, as authoritative sources and attempted to reconcile them where they perceived them to be in conflict.

III. The *Opus imperfectum in Matthaeum*: The Church Concludes Commercial Activity Can Never Please God

The *Opus imperfectum* answers the question "can a merchant please God?" with a rather emphatic "no." In commenting on the cleansing of the Temple by Jesus in Matthew 21:12,[55] the author of the *Opus imperfectum* makes the following oft-quoted[56] statement: "*Homo mercator vix aut numquam potest Deo placere,*"[57] or, "a merchant can never or almost never please God."[58] The full context of the quote reads as follows:

> This means that a merchant can never or almost never please God. Therefore, no Christian should be a merchant. Or, if he wishes to be a merchant, let him be thrown out of the church according to the saying of the prophet, "Because I have not known bargaining I will enter into the Kingdom of Heaven." . . . He who buys and sells cannot be free of lies and perjury: for it is necessary that one of the merchants swear that the thing he is buying is not worth its price, while the other swear [sic] that the thing he is selling is worth more than the sale price. Nor is the property of the merchants stable. It is either destroyed while the merchant is still alive, or it is dissipated by bad heirs or it is inherited by outsiders and enemies. Nothing that is collected evilly can come to any good.[59]

Here is a sweeping statement appearing to condemn all commercial activity by arguing that anyone who buys and sells cannot be free of the sin of lying. Such a statement does indeed envisage an attitude "towards commerce not merely passive but actively hostile."[60]

Of course, the logical question then becomes "who is a merchant?" and therefore subject to such awesome judgment. Pseudo-Chrysostom raises, and then answers, this question. In relevant part, he states:

---

[55]"And Jesus entered the temple and drove out all those who were buying and selling in the temple, and overturned the tables of the money changers and the seats of those who were selling doves." *Matthew* 21:12.

[56] *Id.* at 336, 618 n.5. The Scholastics frequently quoted and discussed this statement. *See, e.g.,* Thomas Aquinas Summa Theologica, ST II-II, Qu. 77, Art. 4, Obj. 1. However, as noted earlier, they wrongly attributed it to St. John Chrysostom.

[57] Opus imperfectum in Matthaeum (Patrologia Gaeca, J.P. Milgne (Paris: 1857-1886), 56:839).

[58] LAIOU, *supra* note [50], at 247 (quoting *Opus imperfectum* (PG 56:839).

[59] LAIOU, *supra* note [50], at 247-48 (quoting *Opus imperfectum* (PG 56:839-840)) (emphasis added).

[60] BERMAN, *supra* note [2], at 336 (quoting HENRI PIRENNE, ECONOMIC AND SOCIAL HISTORY OF MEDIEVAL EUROPE 48-49 (Harcourt Brace 1937)).

He who buys a thing not so as to sell it in the same unchanged and complete form but rather in order to work with it, he is not a merchant, for he is selling not the thing itself but rather his own work: that is to say, *if one sells a thing whose value lies not in the thing itself but rather in the work he has put in it, that is not commerce. But he who buys a thing so as to resell it complete and unchanged and thus realize a profit, he is a merchant who was thrown out of the Temple of the Lord.* Of all merchants the most accursed is the usurer. For, if he who buys in order to resell is a merchant, and accursed, how much more accursed is he who gives at interest money that he has not bought but that has been given him by God?[61]

Thus, the author of *Opus imperfectum* argues that someone who adds value to a thing by adding his own labor is not a merchant. The cobbler, for example, is not a merchant for having bought the raw materials that he will fashion into shoes and then sell. By contrast, the middleman, retailer, or "pure" or "true" merchant who travels to one town to buy shoes from a cobbler there for sale in another town "is a merchant who [should be] thrown out of the Temple of the Lord" and is accursed.[62] Consequently, the true merchant, defined by Pseudo-Chrysostom as one who "buy[s] cheap in order to sell dear,"[63] cannot please God.

However, the author's statements appear to be somewhat inconsistent. He first states that one engaging in buying and selling cannot do so without the sin of lying. Then, in defining who qualifies as a merchant, he asserts that a craftsman, such as the cobbler in the previous paragraph, who adds value by his labor to goods, is not a merchant. Certainly, the cobbler and similar craftsman engage in buying and selling, but they are not by this fact alone condemned as merchants because they add value to the goods with their labor. Accordingly, the cobbler's buying and selling is permissible because he is a craftsman and not a merchant. Pseudo-Chrysostom's definition of "merchant" serves, to some extent, as a limit on the rigorous teaching of this section of the *Opus imperfectum* by restricting it essentially to the pure merchant. The commercial activity seen as sinful by Pseudo-Chrysostom is retailing, serving as a middleman, importing, and like activities that involve of necessity buying with the intention of reselling and at a dearer price.

---

[61] LAIOU, *supra* note 62, at 248 (quoting *Opus imperfectum* (PG 56:840)) (emphasis added).

[62] *Id.*

[63] *See* LANGHOLM *supra* note [47], at 131.

Still, this limitation of the *Opus imperfectum's* teachings on the subject may have served as little solace to a person in Medieval Europe who most likely understands salvation as coming only through the institutional church. Such a teaching, even given the limit supposed in the preceding, was likely downright terrifying as it suggests the possibility that buying and selling could result in being "thrown out of the church." Being "thrown out of the church" would mean being separated from the means of God's grace in this life and condemned to hell in the life to come. As noted previously, the *Opus imperfectum* was "very influential in western Europe," and, therefore, this undoubtedly worked to discourage commercial activity in general and mercantile activity in particular.[64]

IV. The Scholastics' Reinterpretation of the *Opus imperfectum in Matthaeum*: Just Commercial Activity is Pleasing to God

During the time of the Papal Revolution and thereafter, commercial activity experienced explosive growth.[65] Not surprisingly, many of the Scholastics, who were the church's theologians of the time, began to reinterpret the teachings of the *Opus imperfectum* as it relates to commercial activity.[66] Thomas Aquinas's handling of the teachings of the *Opus imperfectum* in the thirteenth century is illustrative of the

---

[64] A sample of related and similarly terrifying teaching is found in James Q. Whitman, *The Moral Menace of the Roman Law and the Making of Commerce: Some Dutch Evidence*, 105 YALE L.J. 1841 (1996). Professor Whitman discusses a book, entitled *Spiritual Rudder of the Merchant's Ship*, written for merchants by a Dutch preacher named Godfried Udemans. *Id.* at 1855. This book quotes from *Opus imperfectum in Matthaeum* and notes that Aquinas said similar things. Then, it goes on to state the following:

> This, and the like hard and rough manner of speaking, will easily leave the *pious merchant* disturbed in his conscience and make him restless, especially when these passages are printed alongside the words of Sirach, chap. 26, verse 27: *A merchant can scarcely guard himself against doing evil, and a shopkeeper against sinning.*

Id. at 1856 (1996) (quoting GODFRIED UDEMANS, SPIRITUAL RUDDER OF THE MERCHANT'S SHIP 3 (Dordrecht: Fransoys Boels, 1638)).

[65] For example, Professor. Berman states that:

> [I]n the eleventh and twelfth centuries there occurred a rapid expansion of agricultural production and a dramatic increase in the size and number of cities. At the same time, there emerged a new class of professional merchants, who carried on large-scale commercial transactions both in the countryside and in the cities.

BERMAN, *supra* note [2], at 333-34. Further, Professor Berman notes that this period "has been called 'the commercial revolution.'" *Id.* at 335 (quoting from the title and chapter 3 of ROBERT S. LOPEZ, THE COMMERCIAL REVOLUTION OF THE MIDDLE AGES 950-1350 (1972)).

[66] For the response of several Scholastics to these teachings from the *Opus imperfectum*, see generally, LANGHOLM, *supra* note [47], at 102-03, 128-33, 354-55, and 394-95.

beginnings of this reinterpretation of the rather rigorous teachings of the *Opus imperfectum* and is discussed in the following section. That section then discusses the work of Johannes Nider in the fifteenth century, which builds upon the work of Aquinas and other Scholastics and concludes that the just commercial activities of an honorable merchant are not only lawful, but beneficial to society, and therefore, pleasing to God.

[The section omitted here discusses Aquinas' analysis of the *Opus imperfectum* and commercial activity. Aquinas is more positive toward commercial activity, and he tries mightily to reconcile the teachings of the *Opus imperfectum* with a more positive position toward commercial activity. If you would like to read it, or any of the rest of the omitted article, you may find the entire article at: http://www.rodneychrisman.com/articles/.]

Aquinas thus softened the teaching of the *Opus imperfectum* in two ways. First, he asserts that trading, i.e., commercial activity, is not evil in and of itself. Whether it be vice or not is instead determined by the motive behind entering into the transaction and the end to which any gain is put. Second, he asserts that buying at a lower price and selling at a higher price is not always unlawful. This is the case, for instance, in the situation of the "afterwards, and for some reason" buyer-turned-seller, who buys the good for possession, but, "afterwards, and for some reason," decides to sell it and at a higher price than was paid. While the reasons that Aquinas gives to justify the higher price in this situation would apply equally to true merchants, he does not extend his logic that far. Rather, he appears to support the idea that a merchant buying goods for the purpose of resale at a higher price is behaving sinfully.

Aquinas reinterpreted the teachings of the *Opus imperfectum* to make them more favorable to commercial activity, but he stopped short of recognizing commercial activity as good or permitting buying with the express purpose of reselling at a higher price. Although not taking these next logical steps himself, Aquinas's arguments appear to have provided some support for the work of Johannes Nider, a later scholastic who did take these steps. Nider's work, *De Contractibus Mercatorum*[67] or "On the Contracts of Merchants," written in the fifteenth century, is a "guide for conduct that would enable merchants to engage in trade while still being assured that their practices were ethical, or 'just' in the language of the times."[68] Nider does not specifically address the *Opus imperfectum*, but he does specifically address the issue raised by the *Opus imperfectum* and not reinterpreted by Aquinas—whether a merchant may, without danger to

---

[67] NIDER, *supra* note [26]. This is a translation of Nider's original work in Latin, *De Contractibus Mercatorum*, written in approximately 1430 and published in approximately 1468; *see also* [Daniel A.] Wren, [*Medieval or Modern? A Scholastics View of Business Ethics, circa 1430*, 28 JOURNAL OF BUSINESS ETHICS 110 (2000).]

[68] Wren, *supra* note 67, at 117.

his soul, buy a good at a lower price with the express purpose of selling it at a higher price.[69] The *Opus imperfectum* answered this question in the negative, and Aquinas seemed to have agreed, but Nider, assuming certain conditions such as voluntariness and a just price, reached the opposite conclusion.[70]

[In this omitted portion of the article, Nider's position and his extension of Aquinas' arguments are discussed. Nider is even more favorable to just commercial activity than Aquinas is, and he therefore extends the position taken by Aquinas to cover even those just merchants who buy cheap at some point with the sole intent of selling higher later.]

In support of this extension of Aquinas's arguments, Nider relies on grounds very similar to the ones used by Aquinas to justify his "and afterwards, for some reason" buyer-turned-seller. Nider states "that a merchant of the type just described [i.e., the merchant buying in order to sell at a higher price] can, in proportion to his diligence, prudence, and risks, lawfully receive in exchange" a profit.[71] Nider continues by noting that "it is right for everyone serving the commonwealth by honest work to live honorably by his toil."[72] Therefore, Nider concludes "whoever imports or [maintains an inventory of] goods honorably and usefully serves the commonwealth and, therefore, stands justified in profiting thereby."[73] Nider, with reasons similar to those of Aquinas, justifies this profit as a reward for the merchant's "diligence, prudence, and risks" and his costs of importing and housing such goods.[74]

Thus, by the fifteenth century, Nider reached a conclusion nearly diametrically opposed to the one reached by the author of the *Opus imperfectum*. Pseudo-Chrysostom's position is that no true merchant can honor God, and he defines a merchant as one who buys cheap and sells dear. Nider, on the other hand, concluded that a true merchant dealing justly in "lawful, honorable, and useful goods," far from being "thrown out of the Temple of the Lord," is instead useful to society and justified in earning a reasonable profit from his commercial activities.

---

[69] *Id.* at 38-54.

[70] *Id.*

[71] [NIDER, *supra* note 26,] at 39. Nider develops this more fully in his discussion of the value of goods. For example, he states that:

> Such businessmen may properly charge more than their actual costs because of the expenses, exertions, cares, qualities of industry, risks, and other reasonable engagements or burdens which they undergo in bringing together things useful to men or in preserving or setting out necessary things in the common market place, and because they remain [there] in order that anyone in need may promptly have such goods.

Id. at 30-31.

[72] *Id.* at 39.

[73] *Id.*

[74] *Id.* at 30-31, 39.

Further, with only minor extrapolation, Nider's position is that the merchant engaged in just commercial activity is pleasing to God and that the commercial activity itself is useful to society; therefore, the merchant and the commercial activity are good. Rather than viewing the work of the just merchant as merely neutral as Aquinas did, Nider describes it as "honest work," "honorabl[e]," and a useful service to society.[75] *On the Contracts of Merchants* does not contemplate that commercial activity itself is a danger to the merchant's soul—the danger lies in unjust commercial activity, characterized by the sins of avarice and deceit.[76] Rather, *On the Contracts of Merchants* is written to presumably pious merchants who desire to ply their trade honorably and in a way pleasing to God and written with the express purpose of providing them with guidelines whereby they may do just that. Thus, a fair conclusion is that Nider viewed just commercial activity as a good thing and the pious merchant engaged therein as pleasing to God.

By contrast, the *Opus imperfectum* stood for the propositions that a merchant can almost never please God and commercial activity is almost always evil. This represented the church's position for much of the medieval period. However, by the fifteenth century, the Scholastics, as demonstrated by the work of Nider, had entirely reinterpreted this teaching. Nider, representing his understanding of the church's teachings,[77] agrees that an unjust merchant can never please God, but a merchant engaged in just commercial activity is understood by Nider as pleasing to God. Additionally, the just commercial activity of that merchant is seen as useful to society and therefore basically good.

Thus, at least by the conclusion of the Scholastic period (and to a large degree much earlier in the period), the Church's teachings on commercial activity can be summarized as just commercial activity is pleasing to God. This idea, that "the economic activities of merchants, like other secular activities, were no longer to be considered as necessarily 'a danger to salvation'; on the contrary, they were considered to be a path to salvation, if carried on according to the principles laid down by the church."[78] These principles—foundational among which is the idea that just commercial activity is pleasing to God—formed the basis for the

---

[75] [*Id.*] at 39.

[76] *Id.* at 38-54.

[77] In the introduction to *On the Contracts of Merchants*, the editor writes "that Friar Nider's primary purpose for writing *De Contractibus Mercatorum* was to provide a moral guide to those" engaged in commercial activity. The guide was written "in terms of the author's understanding of the accepted views of the Roman Catholic Church of Western Europe." Thus, "[t]he innumerable references to that which is 'just,' or 'right,' or 'lawful,' . . . should be read as intended primarily to remind the reader that worldly action should be judged by churchly standards of morality." NIDER, *supra* note [26], at viii.

[78] BERMAN, *supra* note [2], at 339.

mercantile law, "a system of law based on the will of God as manifested in reason and conscience." [79]   Departing from this understanding of commercial law has necessarily led to a lack of coherence and consistency in commercial law jurisprudence. Perhaps a return to it can restore these essential characteristics.

V. Toward a Law-of-Nature Commercial Law Jurisprudence Based Upon the Foundational Principle that Just Commercial Activity is Pleasing to God

In another time, when people thought much differently, Justice Story of the United States Supreme Court could write of such a thing as "the general principles and doctrines of commercial jurisprudence" and general "principles of commercial law."[80]   These general principles of commercial law where thought to be the same for all people for all time in all places:

> The law respecting [commercial activity] may be truly declared in the languages of Cicero, adopted by Lord Mansfield in *Luke* v. *Lyde*, 2 Burr. 883, 887, to be in a great measure, not the law of a single country only, but of the commercial world. *Non erit alia lex Romae, alia Athenis; alia nunc, alia posthac; sed et apud omnes gentes, et omni tempore una eademque lex obtinebit.*[81]

For centuries, courts in the West would reason from these general principles of commercial law to the particular facts of a given case. The departure from this way of thinking has greatly contributed to the current incomprehensibility of law and the related cynicism toward and contempt of law in the West. Given the disastrous results of this change in jurisprudential thinking, perhaps a return to early models and ways of thinking is in order.[82]

---

[79] *Id.*

[80] Swift v. Tyson, 41 U.S. 1, 18-19 (1842), *overruled by* Erie R. Co. v. Tompkins, 304 U.S. 64, 79-80 (1938).

[81] *Id.* at 19. The quoted phrase from Cicero can be translated "nor will there be one law in Rome, another in Athens, another now, another in the future, but one law eternal and immutable will bind together all nations of all times." III MARCUS TULLIUS CICERO, DE RE PUBLICA 22 (James E.G. Zetzel) (1995).

[82] Livy makes just such a suggestion in THE EARLY HISTORY OF ROME. He writes:
I invite the reader's attention to much more serious consideration of the kind of lives our ancestors lived, of who were the men, and what the means both in politics and war by which Rome's power was first acquired and subsequently expanded; I would then have him trace the process of our moral decline, to watch, first, the sinking of the foundations of our morality as the old teaching was allowed to lapse, then the rapidly

Such a return should begin with the recognition that there are general principles of commercial law that are knowable and can serve as the basis for a jurisprudence of commercial law. Further, as the Scholastics eventually concluded, a foundational general principle of commercial law is that just commercial activity is a good thing.

[This omitted portion of the article discusses the fact that "there are general principles of law that are knowable and can serve as a basis for legal analysis," in general and in particular discusses Dean Jeffrey Tuomala's magnificent article *Marbury v. Madison and the Foundation of Law*, 4 LIBERTY U. L. REV. 297 (2010). I would highly recommend this article to every Christian legal professional. This portion of the article then concludes that the bankruptcy of the current way of "doing law" requires a return to the earlier Christian model that undergirded the Western legal tradition for centuries.]

Therefore, a return to the other model of thought about the law is warranted. Pursuant to that model of legal thought, such general principles of law really do exist, as evidenced by Justice Story's statements in *Swift v. Tyson* quoted earlier. Further, Christianity forms the basis for these general principles of commercial law. As Justice Story wrote elsewhere, "[t]here never has been a period, in which the common law did not recognize recognise Christianity as lying at its foundations."[83] In a similar vein, Dean Tuomala, writing of Justice Story's opinion in *Swift*, states that in *Swift* Justice Story

---

increasing disintegration, then the final collapse of the whole edifice, and the dark dawning of our modern day when we can neither endure our vices nor face the remedies needed to cure them. The study of history is the best medicine for a sick mind; for in history you have a record of the infinite variety of human experience plainly set out for all to see; and in that record you can find for yourself and your country both examples and warning; fine things to take as models, base things, rotten through and through, to avoid.

LIVY, THE EARLY HISTORY OF ROME 30 (Aubrey de Selincourt trans., Penguin Classics 2002). The prophet Jeremiah suggests a similar remedy for the people of Judah when he writes, "Thus says the Lord, 'Stand by the ways and see and ask for the ancients paths, Where the good way is, and walk in it; And you will find rest for your souls." *Jeremiah* 6:16. This is not a romantic imagining that the "the good old days" were much better. *Ecclesiastes* 7:10. Rather, it is an understanding that, when one's way has been lost, it is often helpful to return to the place in the road where the wrong turn was made.

[83] Joseph Story, Address Discourse Pronounced upon the Inauguration of the Author, as Dane Professor of Law in Harvard University, August 25th, 1829, in THE LEGAL MIND IN AMERICA: FROM INDEPENDENCE TO THE CIVIL WAR 178 (Perry Miller ed., Cornell Univ. Press 1969) (1962) ("One of the beautiful boasts of our [United States] municipal jurisprudence is, that Christianity is part of the Common Law, from which it seeks the sanction of its rights, and by which it endeavours to regulate its doctrines . . . . There never has been a period in which the common law did not recognise Christianity as lying at its foundations.").

cited opinions from multiple jurisdictions and different periods in history, not as evidence of some broader social custom, but as evidence of what the law of God is on a particular matter of commercial law. The *Swift* opinion embodies the view that law is "permanent, uniform and universal." It does not change; it applies to everyone equally; and it applies in every part of the world. This was Blackstone's view of the common law, and it was also Lord Coke's view of the common law.[84]

In an important footnote, Dean Tuomala further elucidates this "permanent, uniform, and universal nature of the law to which Story alluded in *Swift*" by setting forth the entire context, from Cicero, of the Latin phrase quoted by Justice Story in *Swift*. It reads:

[L]aw in the proper sense is right reason in harmony with nature. It is spread through the whole human community, unchanging and eternal, calling people to their duty by its commands and deterring them from wrong-doing by its prohibitions. When it addresses a good man, its commands and prohibitions are never in vain; but those same commands and prohibitions have no effect on the wicked. This law cannot be countermanded, nor can it be in any way amended, nor can it be totally rescinded. We cannot be exempted from this law by any decree of the Senate or the people; nor do we need anyone else to expound or explain it. *There will not be one such law in Rome and another in Athens, one now and another in the future, but all peoples at all time will be embraced by a single and eternal and unchangeable law*; and there will be, as it were, one lord and master of us all—the [G]od who is the author, proposer, and interpreter of that law.[85]

The Law of God provides the general principles of commercial law. It is only from these general principles of commercial law that one can hope to develop a consistent and coherent commercial law jurisprudence.

---

[84] [Jeffrey] Tuomala, [Marbury v. Madison *and the Foundations of Law*, 4 LIBERTY U. L. REV. 297,] 318 [(2010)] (footnotes omitted) [Dean Tuomala's article is absolutely fantastic and I highly recommend it to you.]; *see also* SMITH, *supra* note [5], 45-48 ("Blackstone and Story were, after all, heirs of a worldview that assumed that God was real—*more* real than anything else, in fact, or *necessarily* rather than just *contingently* real—and had created the universe according to a providential plan. This view had important implications for the nature of law.").

[85] *Id.* at 318 n.106 (quoting Cicero, *The Republic, in* THE REPUBLIC AND THE LAWS 68-69 (Niall Rudd trans., 1998) (emphasis added)).

It is here, then, that the church's view of commercial activity becomes so very important. The church's historic view of commercial activity assists in determining the Law of God with regard to commercial activity and therefore the general principles of commercial law. Certainly, the church can be in error with regard to a particular teaching, as it was for some time when it concluded that commercial activity, and therefore merchants, could not please God.[86] As this Article demonstrated herein, however, the Scholastics moved the church away from this teaching, eventually concluding that just commercial activity is pleasing to God. This teaching is consistent with the Bible.

The Bible assumes private property rights and a market economy.[87] Further, the Bible never condemns commercial activity in and of itself nor does it forbid Christians from becoming merchants.[88] The Bible does, however, have much to say about unjust commercial activity.[89] For

---

[86] Obviously, the author is a Protestant. Therefore, he adheres to *Sola Scriptura*—a Latin phrase from the Reformation that literally means "scripture alone" and summarizes the Reformation teaching "that Scripture alone is absolutely authoritative for doctrine and practice, and following Scripture alone is sufficient to please God in all things." THE ESV STUDY BIBLE 2614 (Wheaton, IL: Crossway Bibles, 2008). Popes, councils, the church fathers, and all other mortal men may err, but the Bible is infallible and is therefore the standard by which all things are to be judged. *See, e.g., Westminster Confession of Faith*, Chapter 1. For more on the differences between the Roman Catholic and Protestant approaches to law, *see* Jeffrey C. Tuomala, *Book Review: Robert George's* The Class of Orthoxies: Law, Religion, and Morality in Crisis, 3 LIBERTY U. L. REV. 77 (2009).

[87] The command found in the Ten Commandments and elsewhere in the Bible not to steal makes sense only in light of private ownership rights in property. *See, e.g., Exodus* 20:15 and 22:1-4, *Leviticus* 19:11, *Deuteronomy* 5:19, *Proverbs* 30:9, *Matthew* 19:18, *Romans* 13:9, and *Ephesians* 4:28. Further, the commands against coveting the property of another imply the same thing. *See, e.g., Exodus* 20:17, *Deuteronomy* 5:21, *Matthew* 5:28, *Romans* 7:7 and 13:9, *Ephesians* 5:3-5, and *Colossians* 3:5; *see also* WAYNE GRUDEM, BUSINESS FOR THE GLORY OF GOD: THE BIBLE'S TEACHING ON THE MORAL GOODNESS OF BUSINESS 19-24 (2003) (discussing the goodness of ownership.)

Further, there are a number of passages in the Bible that condemn financial unfairness in the market, which of course assumes that there is such a thing as a market. *See, e.g., Leviticus* 19:35-36, *Deuteronomy* 25:13-15, *Proverbs* 11:1, 16:11, 20:10 and 23, *Micah* 6:11, and *Hosea* 12:7. Accordingly, the Bible implicitly affirms the free market by condemning those who act deceitfully in that market without condemning the market itself. *See also* GRUDEM, *supra* note [87], 61-66 (discussing the goodness of competition.)

[88] In addition to the passages listed in the previous footnote, there are a number of craftsman and merchants in the New Testament who are never condemned for being merchants and are never commanded to seek out a different way of life. *See, e.g., Acts* 16:14-15, 40 (Lydia, who was a purple cloth merchant) and 18:2-3 (Aquila, Priscilla, and even the Apostle Paul, who were tentmakers.); *see also* GRUDEM, *supra* note [87], 35-45 (discussing the goodness of commercial transactions and profit).

[89] *See, e.g., Leviticus* 19:35-36; *Deuteronomy* 25:13-15; *Proverbs* 11:1, 16:11, 20:10, 20:23; *Micah* 6:11; *Hosea* 12:7.

example, it condemns unjust weights and measures,[90] forbids certain types of security interests that would be particularly harmful to the poor,[91] and demands respect for debtors in the repossession of collateral that is located in a dwelling,[92] just to name a few. Taken together, these passages establish a foundational general principle of commercial law—that just commercial activity is pleasing to God and is a good thing.

This foundational principle would do much to begin unifying and organizing thought regarding commercial law. As an initial matter, it provides a deeper meaning to the oft-stated comment that "commercial law is merely the rules by which business people do their work." Commercial law is such a set of rules because it serves the interests of those engaged in commerce, but that is not all that it is. Instead, it provides the necessary legal framework to encourage just commercial activity and to discourage and punish unjust commercial activity. As noted here, this just commercial activity is pleasing to God and beneficial to society. Therefore, a legal framework that encouraged such activity, while taking adequate precautions against unjust practices, is a good thing and much more than just a collection of rules for the benefit of merchants.

[This omitted portion of the article makes application of this approach to the law of secured transactions, which is a part of commercial law and is largely embodied in the Uniform Commercial Code Article 9.]

VI. Conclusion

In conclusion, commercial law in modern times has lacked any coherent and consistent jurisprudential understanding. Commercial law has often been understood as little more than a set of rules, promulgated by some sovereign, to govern the affairs of business people and provide them a clear framework within which to act. These rules have been, therefore, viewed as perhaps little more than arbitrary guidelines based on an implicit assumption that one set of rules would be just as good as any other.

This Article suggests, however, that perhaps a law-of-nature approach to commercial law jurisprudence could provide a coherent and

---

[90] *Leviticus* 19:35-36; *Deuteronomy* 25:13-15; *Proverbs* 11:1, 16:11, 20:10, 20:23; *Micah* 6:11; *Hosea* 12:7.

[91] *See Deuteronomy* 24:6 (forbidding the pledge of a handmill or upper millstone, which would leave the debtor without a way to grind grain for bread), 24:12-13 (requiring that a poor man's cloak, if taken in pledge, be returned to him at night so that he can sleep in it and be warmed), *Exodus* 22:25-27 (same), and *Deuteronomy* 24:17 (forbidding the pledge of a widow's garment).

[92] *Deuteronomy* 24:10-11 (forbidding entrance into a debtor's house to take a pledge, requiring instead that the creditor remain outside and wait for the debtor to bring it out).

consistent understanding of commercial law. To develop such an understanding, this Article looks to the church's historic view of commercial activity. Moving into the Medieval period, the church had developed a very negative view toward commercial activity. This view is exemplified by the *Opus imperfectum*, which declared that a merchant can never or almost never please God.

This negative view of commercial activity largely held sway in the church until the Papal Revolution. During this time, the Scholastics began to reinterpret the teachings of the *Opus imperfectum* to bring them more into line with the actual teachings of the Bible, finally reaching the conclusion, just before the period of the Reformation, that just commercial activity is pleasing to God. This conclusion can then serve as a foundational general principle of commercial law upon which a coherent and consistent jurisprudence of commercial law can be developed. That work is well beyond the scope of this Article, but perhaps this Article can serve as an initial step toward that laudable goal.

NOTES AND QUESTIONS

1. What Do You Think? What do you think? Are you convinced that just commercial activity is a good thing? Why or why not? If it is a good thing, should the legal system encourage it? How would it do that?

_____

_____

_____

_____

_____

2. But What about all the Bad Stuff? Undoubtedly there are lots of opportunities for evil and sin in commercial activity? The church seems to have always recognized this, and we don't need to look further than the scandals and crashes of our day to see it in our times. However, just because something can be perverted to evil doesn't mean that the thing itself is evil, right? How would you respond to someone who says that commercial activity should be eliminated because it gives rise to all of these opportunities for sin?

_____

_____

_____

_____

_____

_____

3. Implications for the Law? If the excerpted article above is correct, and just commercial activity is a good thing, what are some implications for the legal system? How should it look different if it were based on this fundamental assumption?

_____

_____

_____

_____

_____

_____

CHAPTER 8
IS UNCONSCIONABILITY A JUST LEGAL DOCTRINE?

Jones v. Star Credit Corp.
298 N.Y.S.2d 264, 6 UCC Rep.Serv. 76 (1969)

On August 31, 1965 the plaintiffs, who are welfare recipients, agreed to purchase a home freezer unit for $900 as the result of a visit from a salesman representing Your Shop At Home Service, Inc. With the addition of the time credit charges, credit life insurance, credit property insurance, and sales tax, the purchase price totaled $1,234.80. Thus far the plaintiffs have paid $619.88 toward their purchase. The defendant claims that with various added credit charges paid for an extension of time there is a balance of $819.81 still due from the plaintiffs. The uncontroverted proof at the trial established that the freezer unit, when purchased, had a maximum retail value of approximately $300. The question is whether this transaction and the resulting contract could be considered unconscionable within the meaning of Section 2—302 of the Uniform Commercial Code which provides in part:

(1) If the court as a matter of law finds the contract or any clause of the contract to have been unconscionable at the time it was made the court may refuse to enforce the contract, or it may enforce the remainder of the contract without the unconscionable clause, or it may so limit the application of any unconscionable clause as to avoid any unconscionable result.

(2) When it is claimed or appears to the court that the contract or any clause thereof may be unconscionable the parties shall be afforded a reasonable opportunity to present evidence as to its commercial setting, purpose and effect to aid the court in making the determination.

There was a time when the shield of 'caveat emptor' would protect the most unscrupulous in the marketplace—a time when the law, in granting parties unbridled latitude to make their own contracts, allowed exploitive and callous practices which shocked the conscience of both legislative bodies and the courts.

The effort to eliminate these practices has continued to pose a difficult problem. On the one hand it is necessary to recognize the importance of preserving the integrity of agreements and the fundamental right of parties to deal, trade, bargain, and contract. On the other hand there is the concern for the uneducated and often illiterate individual who is the victim of gross inequality of bargaining power, usually the poorest members of the community.

Concern for the protection of these consumers against overreaching by the small but hardy breed of merchants who would prey on them is not novel. The dangers of inequality of bargaining power were vaguely recognized in the early English common law when Lord Hardwicke wrote of a fraud, which "may be apparent from the intrinsic nature and subject of the bargain itself; such as no man in his senses and not under delusion would make." The English authorities on this subject were discussed in Hume v. United States, 132 U.S. 406, 411, 10 S.Ct. 134, 136, 33 L.Ed. 393 (1889) where the United States Supreme Court characterized these as "cases in which one party took advantage of the other's ignorance of arithmetic to impose upon him, and the fraud was apparent from the face of the contracts."

The law is beginning to fight back against those who once took advantage of the poor and illiterate without risk of either exposure or interference. From the common law doctrine of intrinsic fraud we have, over the years, developed common and statutory law which tells not only the buyer but also the seller to beware. This body of laws recognizes the importance of a free enterprise system but at the same time will provide the legal armor to protect and safeguard the prospective victim from the harshness of an unconscionable contract.

Section 2—302 of the Uniform Commercial Code enacts the moral sense of the community into the law of commercial transactions. It authorizes the court to find, as a matter of law, that a contract or a clause of a contract was "unconscionable at the time it was made," and upon so finding the court may refuse to enforce the contract, excise the objectionable clause or limit the application of the clause to avoid an unconscionable result. "The principle," states the Official Comment to this section, "is one of the prevention of oppression and unfair surprise." It permits a court to accomplish directly what heretofore was often accomplished by construction of language, manipulations of fluid rules of contract law and determinations based upon a presumed public policy.

There is no reason to doubt, moreover, that this section is intended to encompass the price term of an agreement. In addition to the fact that it has already been so applied, the statutory language itself makes it clear that not only a clause of the contract, but the contract *in toto*, may be found unconscionable as a matter of law. Indeed, no other provision of an agreement more intimately touches upon the question of unconscionability than does the term regarding price.

Fraud, in the instant case, is not present; nor is it necessary under the statute. The question which presents itself is whether or not, under the circumstances of this case, the sale of a freezer unit having a retail value of $300 for $900 ($1,439.69 including credit charges and $18 sales tax) is unconscionable as a matter of law. The court believes it is.

Concededly, deciding the issue is substantially easier than explaining it. No doubt, the mathematical disparity between $300, which presumably includes a reasonable profit margin, and $900, which is exorbitant on its face, carries the greatest weight. Credit charges alone exceed by more than $100 the retail value of the freezer. These alone, may be sufficient to sustain the decision. Yet, a caveat is warranted lest we reduce the import of Section 2—302 solely to a mathematical ratio formula. It may, at times, be that; yet it may also be much more. The very limited financial resources of the purchaser, known to the sellers at the time of the sale, is entitled to weight in the balance. Indeed, the value disparity itself leads inevitably to the felt conclusion that knowing advantage was taken of the plaintiffs. In addition, the meaningfulness of choice essential to the making of a contract can be negated by a gross inequality of bargaining power.

There is no question about the necessity and even the desirability of installment sales and the extension of credit. Indeed, there are many, including welfare recipients, who would be deprived of even the most basic conveniences without the use of these devices. Similarly, the retail merchant selling on installment or extending credit is expected to establish a pricing factor which will afford a degree of protection commensurate with the risk of selling to those who might be default prone. However, neither of these accepted premises can clothe the sale of this freezer with respectability.

Support for the court's conclusion will be found in a number of other cases already decided. . . .

One final point remains. The defendant argues that the contract of June 15, 1966, upon which this suit is based, constitutes a financing agreement and not a sales contract. To support its position, it points to the typed words "Refinance of Freezer A/C #6766 and Food A/C #56788" on the agreement and to a letter signed by the plaintiffs requesting refinance of the same items. The request for "refinancing" is typed on the defendant's letterhead. The quoted refinance statement is typed on a form agreement entitled "Star Credit Corporation—Retail Installment Contract." It is signed by the defendant as "seller" and by the purchasers as "buyer." Above the signature of the buyers, they acknowledge "receipt of an executed copy of this RETAIL INSTALLMENT CONTRACT" (capitalization in original). The June 15, 1966 contract by defendant is on exactly the same form as the original contract of August 31, 1965. The original, too, is entitled "Star Credit Corporation—Retail Installment Contract." It is signed, however, by "Your Shop At Home Service, Inc." Printed beneath the signatures is the legend "Duplicate for Star." In substance and effect, the agreement of June 25, 1966 constitutes a novation and replacement of the earlier agreement. It is, in all respects, as it reads, a Retail Installment Contract.

Having already paid more than $600 toward the purchase of this $300 freezer unit, it is apparent that the defendant has already been amply compensated. In accordance with the statute, the application of the payment provision should be limited to amounts already paid by the plaintiffs and the contract be reformed and amended by changing the payments called for therein to equal the amount of payment actually so paid by the plaintiffs.

NOTES AND QUESTIONS

1. What Do You Think? Did the court get it right here? Was there good reason here to ignore the deal into which the parties had apparently voluntarily entered?

_____

_____

_____

_____

_____

_____

2. How Much is Enough (or too Much)? Is it correct to say "that the defendant has already been amply compensated enough?" How does the court know? What if they had only paid $500, or $450, or even $400, would that be enough?

Or, to ask it another way, if $900 was too much to pay, how much would have been enough? Would $700 have been "conscionable"? Again, how does the court (or anyone else for that matter) know?

_____

_____

_____

_____

_____

3. No Meaningful Choice? The court seems to feel that the situation left the plaintiffs with "no meaningful choice." Is this correct? Didn't the plaintiffs have the choice of not entering into the transaction at all?

_____

_____

_____

_____

_____

4. Jephthah's Tragic Vow. The Bible provides us with an example of a tragic vow or promise that had to be fulfilled, despite the horrendous consequences. It is found in *Judges* 11:29-40.

> 29 Then the Spirit of the Lord came upon Jephthah, and he passed over Gilead, and Manasseh, and passed over Mizpeh of Gilead, and from Mizpeh of Gilead he passed over *unto* the children of Ammon. 30 And Jephthah vowed a vow unto the Lord, and said, If thou shalt without fail deliver the children of Ammon into mine hands, 31 Then it shall be, that whatsoever cometh forth of the doors of my house to meet me, when I return in peace from the children of Ammon, shall surely be the Lord's, and I will offer it up for a burnt offering. 32 So Jephthah passed over unto the children of Ammon to fight against them; and the Lord delivered them into his hands. 33 And he smote them from Aroer, even till thou come to Minnith, *even* twenty cities, and unto the plain of the vineyards, with a very great slaughter. Thus the children of Ammon were subdued before the children of Israel.

[34] And Jephthah came to Mizpeh unto his house, and, behold, his daughter came out to meet him with timbrels and with dances: and she *was his* only child; beside her he had neither son nor daughter. [35] And it came to pass, when he saw her, that he rent his clothes, and said, Alas, my daughter! thou hast brought me very low, and thou art one of them that trouble me: for I have opened my mouth unto the Lord, and I cannot go back. [36] And she said unto him, My father, *if* thou hast opened thy mouth unto the Lord, do to me according to that which hath proceeded out of thy mouth; forasmuch as the Lord hath taken vengeance for thee of thine enemies, *even* of the children of Ammon. [37] And she said unto her father, Let this thing be done for me: let me alone two months, that I may go up and down upon the mountains, and bewail my virginity, I and my fellows. [38] And he said, Go. And he sent her away *for* two months: and she went with her companions, and bewailed her virginity upon the mountains. [39] And it came to pass at the end of two months, that she returned unto her father, who did with her *according* to his vow which he had vowed: and she knew no man. And it was a custom in Israel, [40] *That* the daughters of Israel went yearly to lament the daughter of Jephthah the Gileadite four days in a year.[8]

Commentators disagree over whether Jephthah had to actually offer his daughter up as a burnt offering, or whether she simply remained a virgin for all of her life. Either would have been tragic for both. Regardless, it clearly makes the point that vows to God, and by extension vows to our fellowman, should be taken very seriously, even if it is a "bad deal."

Dean Titus argues that: since man is not obligated to make vows or promises to God or his fellowman, i.e., he has freedom to abstain from vows or promises, he is bound by his words when he does make a vow or promise. This is related to the idea of freedom of contract that we discussed earlier. Herbert W. Titus, *God, Man, and Law: The Biblical Principles* 219 (1994). In discussing this idea, Dean Titus addresses Jephthah's tragic vow as follows: "Jephthah's vow to sacrifice the first one out of his house to meet him after victory over Israel's enemy was binding even though its fulfillment required the putting to death of Jephthah's daughter, a clear violation of God's law against murder." *Id.*

This is, admittedly, a very difficult Bible passage to understand. However, it seems to clearly teach the sacredness of promises, if nothing else, in a graphic and tragic way. This teaching lines up with the Bible's

---

[8] The painting that serves as the cover art for this book is of Jephthah being comforted by his daughter. It was completed in 1867 by Sir John Everett Millais.

other teachings on this topic. *See, e.g., Exodus* 20:16, *Leviticus* 19:11, *Psalm* 15:1-4 and 58:3, *Proverbs* 6:16-19, *Ecclesiastes* 5:4-7, *Matthew* 5:33-37, *Ephesians* 4:25, and *Colossians* 3:9. What do you think? Does this Bible story and the related principle that our promises are sacred and must be kept even in very difficult situations shed any light on whether this case was rightly decided?

_____

_____

_____

_____

_____

5. Is this Justice? It is often said that "bad facts make bad law." Certainly, this was a tough deal for the plaintiffs. However, does that fact alone mean that the court was in the right to rule as it did? Did the court consider things that should not be considered when administering justice? *See Exodus* 23:1-9; *Leviticus* 19:15; and *Deuteronomy* 1:16-17.

_____

_____

_____

_____

_____

6. Prof. Bern on Jones v. Star Credit Corp. Prof. Bern used the facts of this case as Illustration 8 in his *Biblical Model* article. His comments are very helpful.

Unconscionability is a defense recognized by both the Uniform Commercial Code and Restatement (Second) of Contracts. Neither provision provides a definition of "unconscionability," and all authorities agree the term is undefinable. The concept is typically said to include "an absence of meaningful choice on the part of one of the parties together with contract terms which are unreasonably favorable to the other party."

Factors of status, behavior and substance often combine in the court's assessment of whether there was an absence of meaningful choice or whether the terms were unduly favorable to one of the parties. In the cases in which the unconscionability defense is asserted, the behavior factor itself is insufficient to raise a defense consistent with Biblical principles. Rather the behavior, (e.g., the sales pitch used, or the way terms were worded or presented in written documents) is usually posited to have significance because of the social, educational or economic status of the promisor, or because of a perceived disparity in the substance of the transaction.

Under the Model analysis, it appears that both the status factor and the substance factor are contrary to Biblical principles. Considering the economic, social, and educational status of the litigants, and favoring the weaker party is inconsistent with the *mishpat* requisite for the proper administration of justice. That feature of impartial and even-handed treatment of all without regard to social or financial status is impossible to implement when the status of the litigants is one of the two most significant factors to consider in applying the defense.

Consideration of the substance of the transaction and whether it appears to be unreasonably one-sided is also improper under the Model analysis. Civil Government does not act within its authority when it dictates directly or indirectly the terms upon which parties can or cannot contract, save to the extent of prohibiting bargains to accomplish purposes antithetical to the creation order. If Civil Government attempts to limit or proscribe the substance of what parties might otherwise independently agree upon in otherwise lawful bargains, it acts not in its authorized role as an avenger against evildoers, but rather in a dominion role which has never been assigned to it.

Civil Government is not the recipient of the dominion-mandate, nor is there anything in Scripture to suggest that it is a better judge of what value an article or service has for an individual than is the individual himself. Yet that is the message communicated when Civil Government interposes its judgment that the individual agreed to pay too much. When Civil Government does so, it sends a very negative message about the worth of the individual, or a category of individuals, i.e., that their personal judgments about the worth of an item and the pleasure it will bring to them are unworthy of recognition by Civil Government. It also sends a clear message that such an individual is not responsible for making improvident stewardship-dominion decisions because the Civil Government, which is acting more in the role of a guardian than an avenger of evil, will relieve him of the obligation that his promise would ordinarily create. In so doing, Civil Government undermines the creation order primacy of self-government, as well as the principle of individual accountability to God for stewardship-dominion decisions.

The combined effect of violation of the *mishpat* requisite (by favoring the poor and weak) and the usurpation of dominion authority suggests that in these instances Civil Government is really endeavoring to compel love by the merchant (by precluding him from collecting the promised amount) rather than to provide redress for evildoing. Although *A*, the ghetto merchant, may be motivated by greed and may be guilty of sin by not acting in a loving way toward *B* in pricing the freezer, his lack of charity is a sin before God alone, and does not in this instance trigger the jurisdiction of Civil Government.

Under the Model analysis, the appropriate inquiry is: has *A*, by setting the price at $900 (plus credit charges) on the freezer and encouraging *B* to purchase it, interfered with *B*'s carrying out his stewardship dominion duties to God? The facts do not suggest that he has. *A* offered *B* the opportunity to make a choice about the freezer. *B* could choose to purchase at the price asked, try to negotiate a better price, or simply not purchase the freezer at all. *A* could not compel *B's* decision. As steward over his resources, *B* had the duty to exercise effective self-government in making that choice.

B's decision, the product of neither misrepresentation nor duress, appears to have been that having the freezer presently would be of more value and benefit to him than having $1,234 in cash available over the next several years to purchase other items or services. If *B*'s decision was not the exercise of good self-government and stewardship-dominion duties, that would be sin for which he is answerable to God. If it was a good exercise of his obligations to God, then God is pleased with his use of promise in this setting. In either case, *B*'s breaking his promise to pay the full amount is not only sin, but also an act of evildoing as to *A* under the principles previously discussed in connection with Illustration 1.

The final point to be made takes us back to the acknowledged inability to define "unconscionability." Apart from all of the other problems with the defense previously addressed, the inherently definitionless nature of the defense makes clear that it represents a statement of feelings rather than a statement of a rule of law. Its standardless character obviously offends the *tsedeq* (righteous moral standard) feature of God's law and thus violates a requisite for human law and its proper administration. There can be no expectation that justice will be done in any case in which that feature is not operative.

Roger Bern, *A Biblical Model for Analysis of Issues of Law and Public Policy: with Illustrative Applications to Contracts, Antitrust, Remedies and Public Policy Issues*, 6 REGENT U. L. REV. 103, 147-150 (1995). Are you convinced by Prof. Bern's arguments that the unconscionability doctrine is actually unlawful from a biblical perspective? Why or why not?

_____

_____

_____

_____

_____

_____

Index

A

Abraham, iii, 27-28
Adam, 3, 55
agreements, 3, 27, 45-47, 64, 96
antitrust, x, 1-2, 15, 56, 63, 104
Aquinas, 81, 83-86

B

bankruptcy, 53-54, 70, **88**
Berman, 66-71, 73-75, 79-81, 83, 86
Bern, 2
Bible, vii, 1, 15, 25, 27, 29, 31, 42, 48, 50, 55, 59, 67-68, 80, 90, 92, 99-101
biblical, vii, x, 1-3, 12, 14-15, 24-25, 31, 40, 42, 59, 61-63, 67, 100-102, 104
Blackstone, 41-42, 70, 89
Burkett, 31-32

C

Calabro, 4-5, 7-9
capacity, xi, 33, 35, 37, 39-42, 61
children, iii, 43-44, 53, 55, 76, 99-100
christianity, 67-68, 77, **88**

Chrysostom

Chrysostom, 78-79, 81-82, 85
Cicero, 76, 87, 89
Colossians, 1, 32, 55, 67, 90, 101
commerce, 30-31, 37, 64, 75-77, 79, 81-83, 91
Congress, 17-18, 46
conscionable, 99
consideration, 6-13, 26, 36, 51, 58, 67-68, 87, 102
Constitution, 14, 20-22, 24, 30

D

David, 56, 75
detriment, 7-11
detrimental, 10-12
detrimentally, 7, 12
Deuteronomy, 12-13, 30, 90-91, 101
Dodson, 33-34, 40

E

Ecclesiastes, 13, 30-31, 55, **88**, 101
economics, ix, 55-57, 59-62, 64, 75, 79
efficiency, 59-60
enforceability, 10
enforceable, 1, 4, 7, 9, 11-13, 30, 51
Ephesians, 1, 31, 55, 90, 101
estopped, 10

U

V

W

CPSIA information can be obtained
at www.ICGtesting.com
Printed in the USA
JSHW052030210523
41984JS00003B/56